I0446386

# The
# SECRET
## of the
# DOUBLE
# PIPELINE

And Other Easy Tips and Tricks for
Having a Better Business, a Nicer
Life, and Making Your Marketing
Make More Money

## BY ROBERT W. BLY

*The Secret of the Double Pipeline —*
*And Other Easy Tips and Tricks for Having a Better Business,*
*a Nicer Life, and Making Your Marketing Make More Money*

by Robert W. Bly

© 2024 Robert W. Bly
Published by CTC Publishing,
a division of the Center for
Technical Communication

*The Secret of the Double Pipeline* is copyrighted 2023 by the Center for Technical Communication. No portion of this manual may be reprinted, reproduced, or distributed in any way without the author's express written permission.

ISBN: 979-8-86-714831-7

## WHAT MY SUBSCRIBERS ARE SAYING....

"Your *Direct Response Letter* has provided me more useful information over this last year than any other subscription I hold. You say more in fewer words than anyone I read. Therefore, each of your posts—regardless the thesis—is a learning event."
— JEFF DONALDSON, Fayetteville, NC

"Bob delivers more value in his e-mail sign-up bonuses than most 'gurus' do in their products!"
— SHAUN EDWARDS, Direct Response Copywriter for Agora UK

"Keep doing what you're doing, you make a difference!"
— NIGEL STRATFORD

"Bob, you are a wealth of knowledge and inspiration. Thank you. Although a little late to the game, I am taking action on the path to a better retirement, which you have been illuminating for some time now!"
— BOB MARTEL

"You are a great copywriter and mentor. Of the many things that I admire from you, two that are critical and stand out with you are:
1: Honesty, 2: Trustworthiness, 3: Authority in your field, 4: Simplicity in teaching what you know."
— MR. P.

"Bob, in my view, you've got a HUGE online rep for honesty and modesty."
— BILL MAKLEY

"I can honestly say that I NEVER have been ripped off buying any of your courses or books! If anything, I've learned a great deal of useful information from you."
— JOHN KIDD

"Bob, just loved this piece, especially the last paragraph. You hit the nail on the head. But you do that a lot. Thanks!"

—ALAN CECILIO

"I've essentially given up on other emails from other marketers. Yours I look forward to because of the unique content and your take on current marketing and copywriting issues. I've been a fan for over 20 years and you just keep getting better with age!"

—TIM PICCIRILLO

This book is dedicated
to David Justiss

# Acknowledgments

Some of the chapters originally appeared as articles and columns in *The Direct Response Letter, Brands United, Writer's Digest,* and my LinkedIn newsletter.

# Table of Contents

# Preface

by Ilise Benun, Marketing-Mentor.com

"The Secret of the Double Pipeline" (see Chapters 3 and 5) is just one of the 87 simple ideas shared in this, Bob Bly's 108th book.

The book is a collection of the most popular essays he's written and published in his *Direct Response Newsletter,* through which he shares not only his newest ideas and opinions, but also his tried and true, proven strategies that stand the test of time.

Bob shares his "secrets" and his best practices from 40+ years as a top copywriter, many with a big helping of attitude, from his perch as a self-proclaimed, card-carrying curmudgeon.

This book is perfect for new copywriters as well as established ones, small business owners, or anyone who wants to know exactly how Bob has managed to achieve such a high level of sustained success and longevity.

He covers everything from copywriting secrets, to marketing and self-promotion strategies, to what to say when someone says something offensive. Plus, he shares his hard-earned lessons about how to get the best projects, how to choose the most satisfying projects and how to deliver the best copy to your clients.

So if you love to write and want to make money writing, this book is for you.

It will not only help you live a more satisfying freelance life, it will also help your clients do better and sell more. That sounds like another double pipeline to me!

But wait! That's not all. It is a superbly readable book with super short chapters and, as an added bonus, you'll learn a lot about Bob by reading this book—including why he doesn't own an Apple watch (see Chapter 4). Enjoy!

# Introduction

For well over a decade, I've published *The Direct Response Letter*, a twice-weekly e-newsletter. Originally I dispensed strictly marketing advice. But then I broadened the scope to encompass more areas of business success and life in general.

Then a problem arose: as I get older, I get crankier and more irritable. I hold to the belief that older people as a rule are correct more often than younger people, because, as Louis CK has observed, their opinions are based on more information.

This increasingly grouchy and cynical attitude began to assert itself in my online essays, which I feared would alienate my subscribers. More and more of my essays became what is known in information marketing as "rants"—complains against the stupidity of the status quo.

But to my great surprise, my subscribers loved these rants and opinionated ramblings—and the more personal they were, the better they loved them.

Once I realized that, I continued to indulge myself. And today, my e-newsletter is probably a 70/30 mixture of personal opinions on important business and life topics vs. straightforward tips on marketing topics.

Is this the best advice in the world on business and life? Probably not, but it is the best I can give you, based on my experience as a marketer, entrepreneur, and writer since 1979. You can read my bio at the back of the book, along with testimonials from my e-newsletter subscribers, to determine whether I am worth listening to.

I continue to write and distribute the essays online, so if you have a question, email it to me and I may, if I feel qualified and able, answer it in a future issue: rwbly@bly.com

Almost all the essays in this new book were first published in my e-newsletter; a few were written for e-newsletters published by my affiliate partners, and a couple in my columns for the trade publications.

I typically place most of my books with mainstream publishing houses and usually eschew self-publishing. But I have self-published this and other collections of my online essays mainly because (a) I don't think a major publishing house would go for them and (b) my subscribers and other readers seem to want them. I'm guessing that since you are reading this one, maybe you do too—and I hope you enjoy it.

In addition, you can get all my future e-mail essays free by signing up for my e-newsletter, *The Direct Response Letter*. When you sign up, you also get 4 free bonus reports totaling 200 pages with a retail value of over $100. Details are on the sign-up page, which you can reach by typing www.bly.com/reports into your browser, and also at the back of this book.

It's my hope that by reading this book, you will in plain and easy-to-read language get advice and ideas that can help you:

- Make and save more money.
- Have greater freedom and control of your life.
- Enjoy meaningful work that you absolutely love.
- Improve your business and personal relationships.
- Become financially secure.
- Do what you want and avoid doing things you don't want to do.

I sincerely believe that even if you only get one good idea for improving any of the areas named above, it will pay back the modest cost of this book tenfold or more—not a bad return on your reading investment.

# CHAPTER 1:

# Why You Should be a "Fiduciary Copywriter"

Billionaire Ken Fisher stresses in his TV commercials that his financial advisory firm, Fisher Investments, are "fiduciaries."

He explains that this requires Fisher to put the client's needs first—even above his own.

Well, I am a fiduciary copywriter.

And I urge you to be one, too.

Because in my humble opinion, being a "fiduciary" copywriter … and putting the client first … is the ultimate secret to long-term freelance copywriting success.

As a fiduciary copywriter, I—like Ken Fisher—put the client's needs, money, and desires above my own.

I always recommend marketing tactics that are most sensible, economical, and profitable for the client—even if it means I will earn a smaller fee as their copywriter and marketing consultant.

For example, the client wants a jumbo, multi-component, expensive direct mail package, and I think a simple and inexpensive postcard will likely do just as well or better, I tell him so—and urge him to do the postcard.

When I get started with a new client, instead of signing them up to commit to a large, long-term, lucrative (for me) engagement right off the bat, I suggest we do a small "pilot project" first.

That way, we can get to know each other. Do we work well together? Does the client like me and my service? Is he satisfied with the final product … and the results I generate for him?

With a pilot project, the client can "kick the tires" before buying the car.

When you put your clients first, 3 things are likely to happen as a result.

First, your success rate goes up. And so your existing clients continue doing business with you.

Second, you gain a reputation as an honest and ethical service provider who, indeed, puts the client first.

Third, with that reputation, more people inquire about your services and want to hire you. So you are more in demand.

Bottom line: instead of costing you money, the "clients-first" approach to freelance copywriting can actually make you more money.

And set you up for a fun and financially rewarding freelance copy-writing career—for however long you want it.

CHAPTER 2:

# Don't Let Snarky Pass

Do you sometimes have people saying things to you that are insulting … offensive … inappropriate … obnoxious … irritating … annoying … snarky … or even downright rude?

And when that happens, are you frustrated—because you don't know how to respond, what to do, or what to say—and so, in essence, the person is getting away with it?

Well, next time this happens, look the person straight in the eye, and say:

*"I want to ask you a question: what was your objective in saying that to me?"*

By doing so, you are openly calling them out on their bad behavior—and quite simply, not letting them get away with it.

If they meant to put you down, you are showing them you are aware of their unseemly behavior—and that it did not work.

Rather than enjoy feeling superior, and puffing themselves up at your expense, they will have achieved the opposite—having been found out—and feel uncomfortable or even embarrassed.

In short, they are not achieving a clear getaway with their with the dig at you they wanted to make.

So next time you don't want to let an offensive comment pass, reply:

"What was your purpose in saying that to me."

This will zip them up pronto.

Warning: Some people may be taken aback when you ask them what their objective was in speaking to you in a certain way.

So use the "what was your objective in saying that to me" technique judiciously and sparingly.

Also, your tone of voice and inflection when saying it should be cool and neutral for best results.

Finally, you use this technique at your own discretion and risk.

Disclaimer: I am not responsible for a punch in the face or any other retaliatory reactions that result.

CHAPTER 3:

# The Secret of the Double Pipeline

TG, a subscriber to my e-newsletter, writes:

"As a regular reader of *The Direct Response Letter*, I appreciate your insights in copywriting and online business.

"Recently you discussed the need to have a "double pipeline" of marketing efforts for your freelance business.

"Namely, to do so much marketing that you don't just get enough inquiries to fill up your lead pipeline ... but instead do twice that amount of marketing, so you get twice as many leads as you need to stay busy.

"But say a freelancer doubles up on their marketing and generates more leads than they can handle?

"What do you propose that freelancer should do with those quality clients that they do not have time to work on?

"It seems that if they just turn those clients away, they lose the income that they could have generated.

"In addition, they may also be turning away a future repeat client, as well as a great source of referrals to new clients.

"So, what is your opinion and solution regarding these concerns?"

Well, to begin with, having twice as many leads as you can handle is a nice problem to have.

What's more, having an overstuffed lead pipeline can actually improve your business in 2 important ways:

First, it ensures you are always busy, always have work, and always have money coming in.

Second, it allows you to pick and choose what clients and projects you decide to take on, and also which projects you are going to pass on.

So you only work with clients you like … on projects that interest you … for fees you feel make you well compensated … and for me, I can't ask for anything more.

As to TG's question about what to do with the prospects you turn away, here are some options:

- **Premium** … charge a premium fee. Or at least don't negotiate on your standard fee. Disclosure: unless a job is an extreme rush, I charge my normal fee.

- **Waiting list** … if the prospect is willing to wait, book their project further out for when you will have time for it.

- **Service alternative** … for instance, if you don't have time to write their copy from scratch, maybe you can fit a quick critique into your schedule. Or, offer consulting, coaching, or mentoring of some sort.

- **Referral** … refer the prospect to a copywriter who does have the time to do the job.

- **Products** … sell one of your books, courses, or another instructional information product to teach them to better write their own copy if you can't do it for them.

CHAPTER 4:

# The Secret of Transparency

In copywriting ... and especially when writing emails to your opt-in subscriber list ...

... "transparency" means telling your readers personal stuff about yourself.

Author James Gleick says transparency is "a watchword and a virtue ... it makes visible what would otherwise be hidden."[1]

"It's important that the reader know and like the author, and you should always strive to make yourself likable in your writing," says writer Gary Provost.

*The benefit of transparency is that it often causes people to like you better ... read what you write more closely ... bond with you on an intellectual and personal level ... and become loyal subscribers—and even fans.*

So, in the pursuit of transparency—a few random facts about me:

- To begin with, I have never been on a cruise—and have no intention of ever doing so. One reason is that food seems to be a big part of the cruising experience. And for me, being offered an endless buffet of great free food is too big a temptation to overeat. Also, ever since COVID reared its ugly head, I lack the desire to be trapped with hundreds of strangers on a floating Petri dish.

- I have never gone to a spa, been in a hot tub, or had a massage— nor will I ever. The reason is simple: I don't want any strangers touching my body. (Though to be fair, if they saw it, they wouldn't want to touch me either.)

- For me, summer is a bummer, because I dislike the hot weather. And with global warming, it seems to me more scorching than ever. If you are a climate denier, you disagree with me. Well, I don't

---

[1] *New York Review of Books*, 8/17/23, p. 42.

know about where you live. But here in NJ, the extreme heat is extremely unpleasant. The New York Times[2] forecast July 2023 would be the hottest month globally since record-keeping began in 1850.

- I miss doing live seminars and speaking from the platform. I always loved giving presentations. What I disliked was the necessary travel. When COVID hit, my speaking gigs went away, and I found to my surprise I now like it that way. My days of airplanes and airports are over. I am not coming back. Yes, I do virtual presentations. I even like doing them. But it's not quite the same.

- Historian David McCullough has said "we live in a coarser, cruder society today." I agree. And the fact that I agree bothers me. I worry that I'm becoming too prudish, too judgmental, and too much of an old prune.

- It drives me a little crazy when people ask me all the time if I watch *Game of Thrones*, Bridgerton, and other series—and then are surprised when I say no. But today, there are a zillion channels with elevendy-billion shows to choose from…there is just too much content to absorb. Also, for me, getting hooked on a streaming series seems an enormous time suck. Although I did it all the way through once, with *The Queen's Gambit*. Because I am a fan of Walter Tevis. And I did watch some of the *Ted Lasso* episodes. Mainly because my son was watching them.

- When I was a kid here in NJ, we had only NBC, CBS, ABC, and channels 5, 9, and 11. From when I was very young, I have fond memories of *The Adventure of Superman, Tobor the 8th Man, Gigantor,* and *Diver Dan*; the latter show featured a fish who smoked cigarettes underwater. Tobor also smoked—uranium cigarettes, for atomic energy.

- I wish I had begged my parents to keep any of the cars we had, in particular mom's two-tone 1958 Pontiac Chief with whitewall tires, and also dad's 1962 Chevy Bel Air, a model of which sits atop a bookcase in my office. Classics that people at car shows have restored to things of beauty.

---

2 *New York Times*, 7/28/23.

- I dislike gadgets, gizmos, bright shiny objects (BSOs), and many things that are overly trendy, hip, and considered cool. Or, if I don't actually dislike a particular glitzy new toy, I am irritated that so many people have flocked to the thing largely because that thing IS new.

- For example, I don't use an iPod, laptop, tablet, or smart phone. My primary phone is a landline that sits on my desk. I do own a cell phone, but rarely use it, and the only thing I know how to do with it is make phone calls—which to me is why I have a phone.

- My computer is a desktop PC with raised keys on the keyboard that click audibly when you type. I use it so much and have had it for so long that the letters and numbers have worn off the top of the keys. But that is not a problem, as I learned to type on a manual typewriter with blank keys.

- Of the three other people living under my roof, two have a $500 Apple Watch, and continually attempt, without success, to convince me I should get one. They point out that with the Apple Watch I could access the internet, speak to Alexa or Siri or whoever, measure my pulse, trade stocks online, perform quant analysis, etc. But the only thing I use a watch for is to tell the time. And my $9 Casio watch does that as well as the Apple—for less than 1/50th the cost.

- I don't want to travel, work on a beach, become a digital nomad, or become an expat living by the ocean. I largely want to spend my days at my desk in my home office, sitting in front of my PC, contentedly clicking away at the keyboard.

In an interview, Barbara Walters once asked Isaac Asimov what he would do if he found out he had only a month to live. "I'd type faster," Asimov answered. My man!

CHAPTER 5:

# Waiting for Godot... in Brooklyn

In *Waiting for Godot*, Samuel Beckett wrote:

"No use struggling. The essential doesn't change. Nothing to be done."

Well, for most of my life, I have, if not quite struggled to, been trying to change one particular thing about me—or at least not to feel too guilty about that thing.

Specifically, I often feel guilty that, basically, mostly what I do is sit on my ass, reading and writing—and not much else.

Now, don't get me wrong.

There are some other things I do besides sit on my ass and type.

Some of them I even like.

But in terms of what I love to do, writing is at the top of the totem pole.

Writing is not just my job or profession.

It's who I am.

I am essentially, first and foremost, a writer—someone whom Joan Didion defined as "a person whose most absorbing and passionate hours are spent arranging words on pieces of paper."

Beckett's assertion is certainty true about me: The essential doesn't change.

However, Beckett also said: "Habit is a great deadener."

And here is where I vigorously disagree with him.

Why?

Well, as I have said, my habit is to write all the time.

Though I do feel guilty and sometimes wish things were different, well—the essential doesn't change—at least not for me.

And mostly I am OK with that.

After all, despite Beckett's claim to the contrary, my writing habit hasn't deadened me in the least.

On the contrary, my addiction to making sentences has brought me endless satisfaction, entertainment, fulfillment, and enjoyment for decades.

Plus, though I certainly am not the most successful writer in the world … far from it …

I certainly have enjoyed my career.

What's more, my writing habit has earned me many millions of dollars over the course of my life.

Allowing me to provide for and take care of my family, which is of utmost importance to me.

So rather than being a deadener, habit has given me a fun and comfortable life.

One more thing …

I included this Beckett bit after stumbling across a shopworn copy of *Waiting for Godot*—which I had not previously read, though had long meant to—in a used book stall on a street corner in Brooklyn —- around the corner from my son's apartment there.

Aside from the play being a great work, what I also liked was that the book was an aging paperback edition printed by Grove in 1954.

Foxing on the pages added to slim volume's character, and the book also had that wonderful smell old paperbacks so often have.

I loved the whole thing, both the book as a work of literature as well as the book as an object—as I do with all the books I own.

# CHAPTER 6

# The ABM Formula: "Always Be Marketing"

Subscriber DC writes:

"My clients are in European countries where they typically have summer holidays lasting weeks and sometimes more than a month.

"I have partially overcome the summer lull by 'massive marketing action' all year. I do some marketing almost every day. "But the 3 months from early June to late August is still a bit of a problem. Only today a Swedish client wished me a great summer, and as in previous years, I now won't hear from her again until September.

"You might have some ideas and it would be great if you could cover this in one of your newsletters."

My difficulty in adding value here is that DC says he already markets every day of the year.

So, he is already practicing my go-to strategy for avoiding lulls in your workload: the "Always Be Marketing" or ABM Formula.

But a common mistake many freelancers make is that they only market when they need more business.

When they are busy, they stop.

Because of that, their lead flow slows or halts.

So when they finish all their current projects, the lead pipeline has dried up—and they have little or no working coming in—and suffer slow periods.

ABM is the best remedy for the crisis-lull-crisis rhythm of freelancing.

Now, as DC, even with ABM, still needs help to protect against summer slowdowns, then he may need to revisit his definition of "massive marketing action."

You see, another common mistake freelancers make is to do just enough marketing so they keep the lead pipeline full enough to generate the amount of business they need, without interruption.

Unfortunately, when some of the leads do not pan out, you may find yourself risking a dry spell.

The solution is to use my "Double Pipeline" strategy.

With this method, you do not merely do just enough marketing to generate the leads you need to maintain a steady cash flow.

You do ***double*** that amount of marketing.

So you end up with 2X more opportunities than you need.

That way, even if as many as half of your leads don't close (unlikely), your dance card is still full, and the potential dry spell avoided.

# CHAPTER 7

# Are Most Online Reviews Fake?

According to an article in the Star Ledger (7/2/23), as much as 30 to 40% of online reviews are fabricated or otherwise not genuine.

Now, that's a problem for me on several fronts—most notably in my customer testimonials and Amazon reviews of my books.

For instance, subscriber JS sent me a snarky email saying I write too much…and that no one wants all this copy and content from me.

I politely replied that, while yes, opinions do vary, not everyone agrees with him—and then sent him this link to a few of my testimonials to support my position:

https://www.bly.com/newsite/Pages/Testimonials.html

He retorted that my so-called "proof" was nonsense, because I obviously made up all these testimonials.

It had never occurred to me he would think that—for the following reasons:

First, fabricating testimonials is illegal.

In fact, the FTC has proposed new regulations to put a stop to fake online reviews, according to an article in ANA Business Marketing SmartBrief (10/2/23).

Second, look at the sheer number of testimonials: to fabricate that many would be an almost Herculean effort on my part—and I'm not that creative!

Third, I like to think I have a small online reputation for being honest and reasonably modest.

And therefore would perhaps be less likely than some other digital marketers to make stuff up.

Of course, using customer testimonials has long been a marketing best practice.

But have we today entered a new era of hyper-skepticism in which testimonials have lost their power, because people do not believe they are real?

Amazon reviews have, in my opinion, exacerbated the skepticism and loss of effectiveness when we display reviews and testimonials of consumers praising our products.

And perhaps with good reason: When I look at reviews of books in my niche—some by authors I know personally—I can clearly see many 5-star reviews that were placed there not by real customers …

… but by people I know for a certainty to be friends, colleagues, employees, relatives, and cohorts of those authors.

That's not playing cricket.

If only one or two "planted" reviews show up occasionally, no big deal.

But the rigging of the Amazon review system has become systemic and pandemic.

Even Facebook is contributing to skyrocketing consumer disgust with and disbelief of advertising claims…

…thanks to the never-ending flood of self-congratulatory, brag-and-boast posts by authors, experts, consultants, and other entrepreneurs.

Outrageous claims like: "My copywriting students all earn 7 figures after taking my course."

Well, maybe—but I suspect at least 2 of those figures are to the right of a decimal point!

Back in the day, before the internet, AL, one of my colleagues who sells money-making instruction, would include images of checks his clients had paid to him.

Now, when we do the internet equivalent by showing screen shots of our online sales reports, we are instantly accused of being crooks.

So, do you agree with my analysis here?

And what, if anything, can we do to combat this new hyper-skepticism … and get consumers to believe our real testimonials and reviews, with honest and true claims?

# CHAPTER 8:

# Choosing Enjoyable and Rewarding Copywriting Assignments

One of the keys to having more fun as a copywriter ... and also writing better copy ... is simply to choose the right projects.

And here are my 7 criteria for choosing copywriting projects that will be the most enjoyable and rewarding to you:

**#1:** The topic of the ad interests you; e.g. oceanography.

**#2:** You are writing an ad about something you like; e.g., dogs or cats.

**#3:** You have first-hand experience related to the proposition of the ad; e.g. you have been a salesperson in a car dealership.

**#4:** You have some training in the topic; e.g., you have gone to trade school.

**#5:** You possess credentials that make you qualified to write about a thing; e.g. you are a certified gemologist.

**#6:** You share some of the same demographics as the target market; e.g. age, location, gender, profession, job title, religion.

**#7:** You have some psychographics in common with the target market; e.g., interests, social status, opinions, activities.

Example: For me personally, I gravitate towards products and services that are somewhat technical and complicated in nature—in part because of my keen interest in science and technology—as well as my engineering degree.

There are several advantages that accrue to you when you select projects that fit the 7 criteria above:

- You'll enjoy your work more.
- You'll write superior copy and content.
- You'll feel good about what you have written.
- Your copy will generate more orders.
- You'll be happier about your work.
- Your clients will be happier with your work.
- You will get more clients and repeat business.
- You will make more money.
- You will smile more!

CHAPTER 9:

# Three Crafty Prospecting Hacks

Here are 3 under-used tactics when prospecting for new business....

### #1: Buy the prospect's product.

Before reaching out to a potential new client, buy and use one of their products.

Then, in addition to identifying yourself as a service provider, you also say "I am one of your customers."

Prospects will be more courteous to you ... and a little more generous with their time and attention ... simply because you are a customer—and not just another vendor pitching them.

### #2: Show tribe membership.

If the company makes products for lefties, and you are left-handed, say so—and point out that you are a member of the target market for what the client is selling.

Or, if the company makes foods or pills for diabetics, and you have diabetes, by all means say so.

Doesn't mean they will definitely hire you, but it gives them one more reason to do so.

### #3: Buy the company's stock.

If the company is publicly traded, and you think it is a good investment, buy a few shares.

Then, in addition to identifying yourself as a service provider, you also say "I am a shareholder."

Once again, prospects will be more courteous to you ... and a little more generous with their time and attention ... simply because you are a stock holder—and not just another vendor pitching them.

CHAPTER 10:

# High-Priced Courses: a Rip-Off?

Subscribe JK told me he had some concerns about buying high-priced online training in the marketing and copywriting niche.

Specifically, he asked me: "Bob, how can I be assured of a good return on my education investment … and not get ripped off … and be certain of achieving the great success and results promised by the course marketers?

The short answer is: You can't.

You see, no one can guarantee your success.

"But," you say, "the course guru guarantees results!"

Yes, except…read the fine print.

In most cases, the guarantee is not that you will succeed.

The guarantee is only that if you do not succeed…

Or are dissatisfied with the program for any other reason…

Or for no reason at all….

The seller will refund your money if you ask for a refund within a specific time period—typically 30 to 90 days.

There are 3 reasons why sellers cannot guarantee their training will make you rich and famous.

- First, not every system of money-making or anything else works for everyone, all the time.

Some things work at some times, and not at other times.

If there was a money-making system that always worked, all the time, for everyone….

And you had it….

Then Bill Gates would be your butler, right?

- Second, effort.

   It's up to the teacher to come up with a system that works and be able to teach it well.

   But the teacher doesn't control or determine how well you execute his system …and how much effort you put into it.

In every endeavor, many students get subpar results because they make a subpar effort.

Doing the work doesn't guarantee your success.

But not doing the work virtually ensures your failure.

- Third, not all students are equal.

   Factors that vary from student to student include intelligence, experience, prior education, personality, time, temperament, and talent.

   None of which the course purveyor has much control of, if any.

   Again, if mega-success in anything was guaranteed 100% of the time, Larry Ellison would be in my driveway washing my Prius.

   Speaking of the Prius, could I have bought a grander car?

   Well, I wouldn't mind having a reconditioned 1958 Pontiac Star Chief—the car my mother had when I was a kid growing up in Paterson, NJ.

   But car guys tell me you shouldn't own a classic car unless you have decent basic car repair skills….which I do not.

   Oh, well. Make mine Toyota, then. I really do like driving a Prius.

# CHAPTER 11

# High-Priced Courses: Part Deux

Recently, I mentioned that my subscriber JK was looking for some guidance.

Specifically, on how to select and get the best value in online courses.

To you and JK, and other purchasers of online courses, I offer these 4 tips:

### #1: Beware the hype.

You already know that many online courses are marketed with hype-driven online copy.

Usually the more expensive the course, the greater the hype.

The problem with super-hype is that it may trigger you to pay an exorbitant price for a course.

Either the course simply isn't worth it—or you can get essentially the same content elsewhere for much less cost.

Here's a rule of thumb for evaluating marketing of online courses and anything else:

If it sounds too good to be true, it probably is.

### #2: Be frugal.

For just getting familiar with and beginning to explore a topic, just buy a good book on the subject; you can probably get one used for under $20 on Amazon.

If the purveyor of a high-priced courses has also written a book on the topic, get and read his book first.

Then if you want a deeper dive, consider previewing or taking his course.

## #3: ROI.

If you are just interested in learning, but not sure whether you will apply the information, stay away from high-priced education—defined arbitrarily as info products costing, let's say, $500 and up.

On the other hand, if you intend to apply the information to making money in your business, how much money do you think it can make you.

Look for an ROI of at least 2:1. That is, if the course costs $5,000, you should be able to generate at least $10,000 in gross revenues using the teachings within a few months of completing the program.

## #4: Get a money-back guarantee of satisfaction.

Spending $5,000 on a course from someone you don't know is a bit of a risky investment.

To protect yourself, only buy courses that come with a money-back guarantee of satisfaction.

Terms vary, but prefer guarantees are:

- Unconditional…no strings attached … you ask for your money back, you get it.
- Longer rather than shorter … 90-day money-back guarantee vs. only 30-day money-back guarantee.
- Backed by a reputable seller … someone you have heard of, is known, or you can vet online.

Is this degree of caution necessary?

In my experience, yes: I hear lots of tales of woes from my readers who say they were ripped off by unscrupulous sellers.

*One more thing….*

Many people have negative experiences with online courses.

They pay a lot of money for the class—often thousands of dollars.

But they don't accomplish what the courses teaches.

And they blame the course.

Well in some cases, they're right.

Here's why….

The course creators teach a system or method that has worked for them.

So they assume it can work for their students.

But that can be a flawed assumption.

You see, the course creators have developed a system that works for them.

The method worked, in large part, because it was tailor-made *by* them—*for* them.

By that, I mean the system they teach precisely matches their skills, aptitudes, personalities, preferences, and mindsets.

But you and I are not them.

So what works for them…may not work for us.

For instance, say a student enrolls in a class "how to network effectively."

If he is extremely introverted, as I am, he might not do well with the program—and fail to master and implement the skills.

But the flaw may not be in the course material or presentation.

It might be that the course provider should screen potential students—to make sure the course is right for them—before enrolling them … but does not.

I do such screening with any of my online master classes costing $5,000 or more—using both an online form and a screening phone call.

But many course creators do not—and will accept any student with the money to pay.

In these cases, the risk is that the students who take the course may have skill sets that are much *different* than those of the instructor who created and teaches the course.

And the more divergent the student and teacher are, the more likely that this divergence could be an impediment to becoming proficient.

Making it much more difficult for the student to learn the material— sometimes for a pursuit for which the student is wholly unsuited.

And of course, failure is sometimes the result.

Bottom line: While it is essential for you as a student to know the course instructor has successfully applied the learnings …

You also want to know that other students who have taken his course have also been able to master, use, and profit from the ideas.

CHAPTER 12:

# Lucky Outliers

In statistics, an outlier is a data point that differs significantly from other observations.

A big problem is the tendency of many people to misinterpret outlier results as proof of a given system or principles, rather than what they really are—which is exceptions to the rule.

You see this in casinos.

A player gets away ahead, and suddenly believes she is God's gift to gamblers.

So she keeps playing, loses everything she made, and then loses even more; this is how casinos make much of their money.

*Motley Fool Wealth Weekly* (6/8/23) says, "We don't make investment decisions based on one quarter's results."

Yet many people do just that.

For instance, a couple I know lost a lot of money in the stock market crash of 2000.

And so they concluded that stocks are too risky, and from then on, assiduously avoided being in the market.

But over the long term, the data show that having your money in the stock market makes you a lot richer than hiding your cash in your mattress; the Dow is in positive territory about 70% of the time.

So in the 21st century, this couple has missed out on huge profits—and, as the saying goes, "left money on the table."

Another example of an outlier is when an attractive (e.g. hot bikini model) or talented (e.g. rapper) youngster attracts a zillion followers on Instagram and hits it big. Kaila Itsines, for instance, is an Instagram influencer with 12 million followers and a $46 million net worth.

For every Instagram millionaire, of course, there are elevendy-billion other young, good-looking people with a gimmick who waste their time playing the Instagram claim to fame game and have nothing to show for it.

The list goes on and on.

The lesson?

Well, just because someone did something that makes you burn with envy, doesn't mean you will be successful doing the same thing.

Taking a plunge simply because someone else struck gold with it doesn't mean you will, too.

One thing some outlier superstars have that their imitators don't take into account is luck.

Wise people know that luck is one of the key reasons why people do or do not succeed—the others being timing, talent, aptitude, brains, skill, persistence, knowledge, study, practice, and hard work.

# CHAPTER 13

# The Subtle Power of Value-Added Copy

Copywriting tip: consider using "value-added" language and phrases whenever possible and appropriate.

"Value-added language" is wording that makes what you are writing about seem much more important, valuable, exclusive, upscale, and desirable than conventional phrasing.

Take for example an on-hold message from Medical Guardian—the "help-I've-fallen-and-I-can't-get-up" alert device).

Conventional phrasing would tell you to hold for a "sales representative."

Better would be to tell the caller to hold for a "customer service rep."

But Medical Guardian says: "Life Safety Consultant."

It's a great value-added turn of phrase because:

…"life" is important.

… people value "safety."

… "consultant" sounds more valuable than a "rep."

Is Medical Guardian exaggerating by calling their phone rep a life safety consultant?

Maybe a little.

But I find it an acceptable—and palatable—degree of puffery.

The rule of thumb is: it's OK to make people think you are perhaps 10% better than you really are.

But usually no more than that.

We call it "looking through rose-colored glasses"—so you present as your best self and maybe a notch beyond that.

When I worked summers in a warehouse, we warehouse workers jokingly called ourselves "logistics consultants."

Which obviously sounded a step or two above our pay grade.

I could have said I was a "trained logistics consultant."

Who trained me? The other warehouse workers, who showed me how to stack boxes high above my head.

The training took about 3 minutes.

The skill—tossing a stack of four boxes so they landed and sit snugly on an existing pile of eight boxes—took a week or so to get the hang of.

But given that I was the shortest guy in the warehouse, it was an essential skill for me to master—which I quickly did.

# CHAPTER 14

# The Best Time to Give Clients Gifts (Hint: It's NOT Xmas)

According to an article in ANA Business Marketing SmartBrief (5/5/23), almost 8 out of 10 B2B decision-makers say receiving gifts from vendors prompted them to take a meeting with that vendor.

But, when is the best time to give that gift?

The majority of business gifts are given to customers during the holiday season.

But actually, Xmas may be the worst time to give a business gift... for two reasons.

First, during the holidays, your customer is overwhelmed by gifts from many of their vendors.

And so yours gets lost in the shuffle.

Has a hard time standing out from the pile of other "spiff" in his mailbox.

As a result, the gift has less impact. And is less noticed. And less appreciated.

Second, when you give your customers a gift even once on Christmas, they come to expect a holiday gift from you every year, automatically—which further diminishes its impact.

So, when is the best time for a vendor to give a business gift to a client, customer, or prospect?

Randomly.

At any time of the year when they are NOT expecting it.

Why?

Because the surprise factor makes your gift stand out more, as it is completely unexpected.

Also, it is likely the only gift they get that day.

So it is enjoyed and appreciated more.

One more thing....

I like to get to know my clients—as people—well.

So when I unexpectedly come across a gift item I think they'd really enjoy...

...I buy and send it to them as a gift on the spur of the moment.

They are extra-delighted because (a) it is custom-selected just for them based on their personal preferences, and (b) they had no reason to think they were going to get anything today.

And I feel extra-delighted too, because my selection of that particular gift for that particular person reflects my connection with them—and even more so when they tell me they loved it.

# CHAPTER 15

# Three Things You MUST Put on Your Home Page

Subscriber KB asked me:

"Out of curiosity, what is your take about having long-form copy on websites for businesses run by one person?

"I know long-form copy works very well when it is captivating, entertaining, and informative for a landing page or sales letter.

"However, sometimes I see people's websites and think the copy is way too long—even when it is written well and holds my attention."

Here's my answer for KB and for you, too....

There are two basic types of websites.

One is the long-form website KB is referring to.

These are most often used to sell online courses, videos, ebooks, coaching, mentoring, and other information products.

They are also effective for products requiring long copy and ordered directly online, such as nutritional supplements and stock newsletters.

Here's as example of one of my long-form sites, promoting a single product—an online video course:

https://bobblylive.com/copywriting-mastery-details-c

But for a small service business, a conventional website may be best.

Here's an example—the website for my freelance copywriting business:

www.bly.com

The keys components of bly.com in particular—and conventional small business websites in general—are:

- **The home page, should tell visitors 3 things—who you are, what you do, and why they should care.**
- Additional pages, one each, on the key topics related to your business, often including an "about" page or bio … services … client list … client testimonials … samples of your work … a contact page where prospects can make an inquiry about using your services.
- A menu, cross-links, any other navigation, and a site architecture that makes it quick and easy to find the information visitors are looking for.
- And whatever else you think you need—typically with a separate page dedicated to each—that convinces the consumer about why they should hire you.

Examples include: videos … media coverage … press releases … case studies … tools … white papers … books … methodology … operating principles … seminars … links … glossary … frequently asked questions … pricing and terms … and guarantees.

CHAPTER 16:

# Selling to Info Junkies

There are some people who love to buy information products—… books, e-books, webinars, memberships, mentoring, coaching, master-classes, conferences, boot camps— only to never take action on any of the advice taught in those products.

We call them "information junkies."

Many of the info products they eagerly consume are on such topics as: starting a business … money making … get rich quick … options trading … investing in stocks … cryptocurrencies … commodities … multi-level marketing … and other "business opportunities."

Common benefits promised in the advertising are: make a lot of money so you can live in a mansion… drive a new Mercedes or Bentley … escape the 9 to 5 rat race … be your own boss … work only an hour a day … all from becoming rich and successful.

Many info marketers promise you can do all this with little or no work, effort, time, or money—which led Joe Karbo to call his mail order course *The Lazy Man's Way to Riches*.

And here's a little secret: some of these same info marketers have a low opinion of their customers.

Specifically, those customers who don't follow the teachings and instruction they have purchased—which is typically the majority of buyers.

The fact is, most info product buyers just sit in their armchairs and read the material … but never put the information to work.

One info publisher, DB, unkindly refers to these buyers "the moron market."

Other info sellers make similarly disparaging remarks.

But I don't—and I don't feel that way about these buyers.

Why not?

Because many people enjoy reading, learning, studying ... books, workshops, master classes ... for the pleasure of it.

What's wrong with that?

You may argue, "But they'll never improve their lives, start a business, or make money from the info products they buy!"

Well...that's up to them, isn't it?

Fact is, they enjoy your info products, and that's all they want.

Self-help, success, and business opportunity learning is just a hobby for them.

Don't they have a right to enjoy that hobby, just as they enjoy other pursuits such as golf, hiking, woodworking, and stamp collecting?

Besides, they might not become options traders or entrepreneurs— but some of the information they absorb may be useful to them in other aspects of their lives....

From managing their money, to gaining useful skills, to doing their jobs better—generating some positive ROI for them after all.

# CHAPTER 17

# Apps Are Crap

A subscriber recently asked me what tools, apps, and resources I use.

Well, the list of tools I use may surprise you ... because there are so few.

Three reasons.

First, I am a Luddite—and as such, resist using new-fangled technologies.

Second, I have assistants who handle the tasks others use tools for ... or, I do those tasks myself, unaided.

Third, my time is much better and more profitably spent writing—not learning apps, software, services, and tools which I have no desire to play with in the first place.

For instance:

- I don't have an ATM card. When I need cash, I go into the bank and get it from a human teller.
- I don't use express self-serve checkout at the supermarket. I always go to a full-service checkout lane with a human cashier.
- Reading. I do not own a Kindle ebook reader. I read paperbound books only.
- Writing. The only writing software I use is Word. No Grammarly, ChatGPT, or Dragon Naturally Speaking.
- AI writing software: none. Having been a full-time writer for over 4 decades, I can write a lot better than ChatGPT, thank you.
- Arithmetic. Okay, I do use an electronic calculator, which was standard equipment for engineering students when I was in college. (As seniors in high school advanced physics, we were probably the last class ever to learn the slide rule.)

- Research. A combination of Google search and outsourcing to my researcher—again, a live human.
- Whiteboard videos. There's good software for doing it yourself. But because my time is better spent on my core business of writing than learning tools, I have a guy for this, too.
- Website and landing page design. No WordPress or HTML for me, thank you. I have a webmaster on retainer.
- Apps. Nope. None except Uber in case of emergencies. But so far, I have never taken an Uber.
- Smartphone. The only thing I use my cell for is phone calls when I am out of the office. In the office, I use the landline on my desk.
- PowerPoint. Outsourced to one of my virtual assistants. I can view PPT slides. But I do not make them. My VA does that for me.

The list goes on and on.

Or, more accurately—it doesn't.

Of course, you may respond to all this by telling me I am an idiot and behind the times—or feel compelled, as so many of my readers do, to make recommendations on software or gadgets. I have no objection if you want to do so. But the chances of me doing what you suggest are slim to none.

# CHAPTER 18

# Positive vs. Negative Thinking

Those who think of me as a crabby curmudgeon will not be shocked to learn that a major New York publishing house once expressed interest in having me write a book for them titled: *The Power of Negative Thinking*.

Now, I am well aware of the benefits of positive thinking. However, the notion that negative thinking is always a bad thing is not always true.

The fact is that skepticism, caution, doubt, and pessimism are sometimes useful as protective tools.

Properly managed, some negative thoughts encourage fact-checking, vetting, debates, deeper examination. and further discussion.

Which in turn can help us avoid mistakes, bad decisions, and other errors in judgement.

For example, in his book *Learned Optimism*, Dr. Martin Seligman points out—correctly, in my view—that pessimists have a more realistic and practical view of the world…and things, situations, and life within it…than do optimists.

So if you unconditionally discount all pessimistic thoughts, notions, and instincts, you risk diminishing your critical thinking powers.

And, in some instances, might be doing so at your peril.

Anyway, back to my book, *The Power of Negative Thinking*.

I liked the book title. I liked the idea.

But I did not know how I would fill a 200-page paperback with useful instructions on the subject.

So, I sat down to write it.

And I wrote the first sentence, which I liked—but didn't go any further.

That first sentence, by the way, was: "If you are a pessimist, you will never be disappointed."

And that's as far as I got.

# CHAPTER 19:

# Multiple Streams of Income

When it comes to their income, many people with traditional 9-to-5 jobs are, metaphorically speaking, riding a unicycle.

Just as a unicycle has one wheel, the average worker has one major stream of income: her paycheck.

If she is fired from her job, she loses most or all of her income—which makes riding her way through life, especially given today's uncertain economy, both difficult and fraught with peril.

Well, as you know, if your unicycle blows its single tire, you as the rider are dead on the road—and you are not going anywhere, anytime soon.

But when you are self-employed, a freelancer, or a business owner, you can achieve greater financial security—by enjoying multiple streams of income.

Having multiple streams of income—especially entrepreneurial and investment—is more like driving an 18-wheeler than a unicycle.

How so?

Well, if an 18-wheeler gets a flat tire, it can still physically keep moving forward—though legally and for safety's sake, you should get the tire changed right away, as soon as you reach the nearest service area.

For instance, as a writer, I have multiple clients—and not just a single boss.

When I had a corporate job, if my boss had fired me, I would have, at least temporarily, lost 100% of my income.

But when you have, say, 10 so clients, and you lose one, you retain 90% or so of your cash flow.

Also, it is easier to find a new client than to find a new full-time job.

As a writer, I have multiple streams of various types of income — including copywriting, freelance writing, books, information products, consulting, coaching, speaking, and training.

So even if I suddenly became unable to write, we could live nicely on, for instance, the passive income cash flow from my info marketing business alone.

Your action steps:

1. Write down a list of possible new income streams you could start earning.

2. Pick one and make it happen.

Follow this advice, and within 12 months you could be making an extra $15,000 to $50,000 or more a year.

## CHAPTER 20:

# Avoiding the "Pension Trap"

I'm 66 years old.

Many of our couple friends are my age.

And a large number have fallen into the "pension trap."

The pension trap is when you work for 40 years.

At a job you tolerate at best.

Or that just bores the crap out of you.

Or at worst, a job you loathe.

The pension-trap guys I know who have retired are proud that they get a pension.

Boast about it.

And some laud it over me.

They say they feel sorry for me that I still "have to" work.

But my reaction to that—which I don't share with them—is....

Why would you work at a job you hate for 3 or 4 decades ... if you had any choice in the matter?

It sounds like a miserable existence to me.

A misery confirmed by endless observation of—and conversation with—numerous friends, neighbors, relatives, and others who are pension slaves.

Me, I'd rather spend my life working in a job I love—which I do, as it happens ... and happily forego a pension in exchange for my freedom from what for me would be akin to indentured slavery.

Also, 3 things many pension slaves don't get and never will....

First, if you love what you do, and would even do it for free, then arguably it isn't really work.

It's enjoyable play.

Second, although not all of us who are self-employed or own small businesses are rich—many of us are quite comfortable—and therefore have no need of a pension.

Third, we actually like or love our work so much, that we do not intend to retire.

Because, as Noel Coward so aptly put it, "Work is more fun than fun."

Now, it is not my desire to make my associates who lived their lives for a pension feel badly.

I just want them to know that I like the path I've taken.

And don't envy them one iota.

# CHAPTER 21

# Nostalgia Sells!

I recently got an email with this subject line:

"Your '75 Fair Lawn High School Yearbook is on sale, Robert."

The company, www.classmates.com, gives you the opportunity to buy a reprint copy of your high school yearbook.

They sell it as a sturdy, laminated hardcover … with heavy glossy pages … and durable printing and binding.

The offer is a $20 discount plus free shipping.

There are two downsells.

You can get your high school yearbook in a cheaper paperback edition.

Or read it for free online.

This promotion from www.classmates.com must be successful, because it runs all the time.

Nostalgia is a hot—and underserved—market.

So let me ask ….

Is there something you, your friends, or your contemporaries are nostalgic about?

Then there may be a ready market for you to sell it online.

Think about it. Could be a new business for you, yes?

At my age of 66, there are many things I think about with fond memories that I might actually like to have again—provided I had more space and was in the mood to collect and accumulate—which sadly, I am not anymore.

A partial list includes: old typewriters ... comic books ... action figures ... toy robots ... steampunk art ... 78 rpm jazz records ... magic tricks ... old chess sets ... science fiction collectibles ... and certain books ... to name just a few.

But please don't send me any of this. As much as I like these things, I don't need more stuff.

CHAPTER 22:

# Why I Won't Jump on a Call With You

Just about every day I get an email from someone I don't know.

Usually either trying to sell me something … or to get me involved with their business in some way … or suggesting we talk to explore opportunities or synergies.

And they usually end their message by suggesting that we "jump on a call" or "book a call."

Well, to quote Dr. Evil from *Austin Powers*: "How about NO, Scott!"

Why not?

Well, my time is limited and valuable.

Yours is too.

So why would I take time out of my busy schedule to speak with someone I don't know … about something I am not familiar with … and have no time or interest in pursuing?

When I get push back, I politely explain that all my time is taken up working with my current clients—who are all paying me for my efforts.

Two other pet peeves about requests to "jump" on calls.

First, for me, Calendly doesn't work, because it allows anyone to book a call, without me first qualifying them.

Also when I do have calls, it is at dates and times mutually acceptable to both parties.

Why? Because people who value time and manage it will set their own schedules—and not allow others to do it for them.

Second, Zoom.

If you and I are going to speak, just call me—or I'll call you—on a regular phone.

I don't need to see your face, good-looking though you may be. And you don't need to see mine.

Also, when I am having calls, I want Word open on my monitor's screen—and not a video of the other person's head—so I can type good notes.

I grudgingly admit that I understand why some people like Zoom for calls with multiple people involved.

But again, I don't need to see their faces; I just need to hear what they are saying. For that, an audio conference line, such as www.freeconferencecall.com, works just fine—at least for me.

Also, because I work at home, my appearance can be a bit slovenly and my office somewhat messy. And with audio only, I don't have to clean up!

# CHAPTER 23

# Are You Price Gouging?

This is a common misconception about free markets and capitalism....

Namely, that you can and should always charge as much as the market will bear.

But, one can argue: well, not always.

For instance, charging exorbitant interest rates is called "usury"—and it is illegal.

We use the term "price gouging" as a negative to describe businesses that charge fees so high that customers feel they are being ripped off.

Has that ever happened to you?

The government's legal definition of price gouging is overcharging when there is a critical and dire short supply of a necessity; e.g., the 2023 baby formula shortage.

The government is also increasingly keeping the cost of medications affordable; e.g., insulin.

Which helps people afford their meds, not get sicker, and stay alive.

And remember infamous pharmacy chief Mark Shkreli?

He was the guy who raised the price of Daraprim, an HIV drug, from $13.50 to $750—about a 5,000% increase ... and later was sentenced for (unrelated) hedge fund fraud.

On the flip side, the other day I saw a TV commercial for a local heating contractor in which the owner proudly said:

"We are dedicated to giving our customers superior service AT A FAIR PRICE."

A fair price means getting paid well for your superior products and services.

But without forcing your customers to miss their mortgage payment—or take a home equity loan—to buy what they need from you.

So....

Do you strive to offer great quality and a good value at a fair price?

Or are you purely a money-extraction machine ... always out to always turn one dollar into ten dollars whenever you can, as fast as you can ... even if it means squeezing blood out of some stones who are your customers?

As for what price to charge, pricing expert GD once told me that, as a service provider, your optimal price should be in the middle of the top third of the range.

He said being in the top third convinced people you must be good at what you do.

And you attract customers who want the best and are happy to pay for it.

If you in the middle of the top third, those customers will see you as premium, yet also fair.

But, if you charge at the very top of the range, you risk being so expensive that even your ideal prospects will hesitate to buy from you—because of your price.

# CHAPTER 24

# Is Direct Mail an Environmental Hazard?

So I picked up a magazine in a doctor's office the other day.

It had an article "End the Mailing Madness."

It was a rant against the evils of direct mail.

The article called for curbing direct mail, based on the fact that direct mail, in a digital age, is an "unsustainable practice."

The article says that over 100 million trees are destroyed each year for junk mail, which also adds one billion pounds of waste to landfills annually.

And yes, direct mail is certainly paper.

But, print magazines, including the one in which this anti-DM article appeared, are *also* made of paper.

So, that being the case, riddle me this....

Why is direct mail, according to the writer, unsustainable—but distributing his magazine on paper is fine with him?

The article also says that "companies likely prefer shoppers to visit their websites rather than go through the expense of printing and mailing bulky catalogs."

Well, that sounds logical. Yet despite the advances of the digital age, businesses still mail about 12 billion catalogs a year. Why do you think they continue to do so?

Subscriber BM answered: "They continue to do so because they are able to find ways to make it profitable. They can also reach markets that are off the web or do not trust it. Otherwise, they would stop because it's expensive."

And subscriber JH notes: "The USPS would collapse overnight without ad mail. And the expanding restrictions to online targeting will swing some of that money back to other media, with mail being the most targeted."

Back in the day, magazines and newspapers routinely slammed direct mail as "junk mail."

Apparently ignoring that many of their subscriptions were generated with ... you guessed it ... direct mail.

Also, many direct marketers said that if direct mail is called "junk mail," then newspaper ads are "junk ads" ... billboards are "junk signage" ... and TV commercials "junk television."

# CHAPTER 25

# Nine Ways to Write Stronger Ad Copy

A major and ongoing topic of debate in copywriting is creativity.

When I got into advertising in the late 1970s, the Madison Avenue ad agencies were dominant—and obsessed with creativity.

Many in the field—as well as hordes of people outside of it—wanted, liked, and preferred TV commercials that were either funny, entertaining, or clever.

But in the digital world, we have analytics that precisely, swiftly, and more easily measure the results of marketing campaigns than back in the day.

And while advertising may require some degree of creative thinking, I see it more as thinking to come up with a big idea for your ad.

And not, as was sometimes the case in general advertising, creativity for creativity's sake.

Here's are 9 factors I think are much more important than creativity for making ads that sell:

- Copy that expresses selling propositions ins a new, fresh. and compelling way.
- Emotional copy that addresses the core reason to buy the product.
- Clear benefits that consumers desire.
- A unique selling proposition to clearly differentiate your product from the competition.
- A big idea making strong claims about the product.
- Proof that backs up your claims—with specifics.
- Enough facts and information to motivate the reader to inquire or buy.

- A call-to-action with an irresistible strong offer.
- A sense of urgency: a reason to respond now instead of later.

You may have your own list of what makes for a good advertisement, and I would welcome seeing it.

# CHAPTER 26:

# Stop Your Bragging!

Are you sick and tired of the endless bragging and boasting by copywriters and info marketers online today?

Some of these blowhards have egos bigger than that huge Chinese balloon, said to be taller than the statue of liberty, shot down off the coast of South Carolina in 2023.

These smug blowhards love nothing more than to crow endlessly about:

… how smart they are.

… how successful they are.

… how great they are.

… how much money they make.

Almost everything they say is couched in the most braggadocious terms possible.

Back in the day, we would say our copy "outperformed" the control—or maybe "beat" the control.

Today, egomaniacal marketers puff up their chests as they endlessly tell us they are "crushing it."

So, you may ask…what's wrong with brag-and-boast?

Well…several things.

To begin with, bragging is unseemly.

Bragging builds the braggart up and makes him feel superior.

While simultaneously making the person you are bragging to feel inferior and bad about themselves.

Second: bragging lacks credibility, because the braggart praising himself is not objective.

For instance, if you say you are a genius, it's a pretty sure bet that you almost certainly are not.

But if *other* people say you are a genius, that makes the claim more credible.

Third, braggarts are prone to exaggeration.

People make outrageous claims on the internet; e.g., "My Program Made Me $2.7 Million in 12 Hours."

Yet they either offer no proof—or else no proof that is believable or the reader can possibly verify.

I sometimes—sarcastically—email these braggarts and warn them not to break their arm while patting themselves on the back.

When I got started in copywriting in the late 1970s, it was perhaps a bit more difficult to make outrageous claims of success, because our marketing was more visible.

Example: If you claimed your latest ad was a "killer," but it only ran once, then the smart marketers would know that in fact it did not work—because if the ad had been profitable, you would have run it multiple times.

Though sales made online are less visible than TV commercials or newspapers, they are not invisible.

So when a regulatory agency calls B.S. on you, the proof of your malfeasance can be found in your e-commerce software logs and on your servers.

Fourth, braggarts have selective blindness: they shout the good stuff from the highest rooftops. But when the news is not so good, they can turn awfully quiet.

Richard Branson, founder of Virgin Orbit satellite launch company, once boasted about how great Virgin Orbit is, saying it could connect 3 billion people who are not yet connected.

But according to an article in *Industrial Equipment News* (3/31/23), Virgin Orbit's star seemed to be shining less brightly, as they laid off about 85% of its workforce—and put all projects on hold.

What's the lesson here for you as a consumer evaluating highfalutin statements and claims from big shots who think perhaps their feces is odorless?

Well, one good rule of thumb for you to follow is: "If it sounds too good to be true, it probably is."

Another problem with making outrageous claims on the internet, such as "My Program Made Me $2.7 Million in 12 Hours," is that if it isn't true, you are lying.

Lying in your advertising is both unethical and illegal. Not a very honorable way for you to make a living, right?

## CHAPTER 27:

# I'm a Believer!

An article in John Forde's e-newsletter *The Copywriter's Roundtable* proclaims:

"It's next to impossible to write convincingly about something you either don't care about, don't believe in, or wouldn't do yourself."

But is that really true? And if it is, what can you do about?

For me the solution is "temporary belief."

This means you convince yourself that the proposition is true ... and the product is wonderful ... during the time you are writing the copy.

Getting into this believer's mindset is the surest way for you to write copy that motivates him to action.

For instance, I know a copywriter, JH, who specializes in writing political fundraising—and takes on both left-leaning Democrats and also right-wing Republicans as clients.

JH explains that, while he is writing copy, he serves as an advocate for his client—just as an attorney is obligated to give his clients the best defense possible.

Now, with some imagination and thought, you can usually see the good in most products and things, and use those to write with enthusiasm about them.

As Joseph Kelly, Eisenhower's speechwriter once said, there is a kernel of interest in everything made my man or God.

You have to find it, rally behind it, and write about it positively and with energy.

(Tip: If possible, buy or borrow and use the product you are writing about. This too can make your copy more specific and credible. And make you like it more.)

Take pickleball as an example.

I don't play. So I'm not naturally excited about it.

But I am empathetic enough to understand and appreciate why people enjoy it—well enough to generate the temporary enthusiasm to write a good pickleball ad.

So yes, by shifting your mindset to a state of temporary enthusiasm, you can write strong copy about things that are normally not in your wheelhouse.

Now, that being said, the temporary belief method is much more difficult when you are tasked with writing copy about something you just don't like.

A product or proposition you find downright unpleasant, objectionable, unethical, or dangerous.

Products and activities you find so distasteful and unappealing that you simply can't muster temporary enthusiasm for them, no matter how hard you try.

In that case, you and the client will both be happier and better off by you turning down the assignment.

For instance, I was asked to do copy to sell a series of hunting books.

I turned it down. Even though it was an interesting assignment and a handsome fee.

Now, I'm not saying hunting is wrong.

But I love animals.

And so the idea of shooting one of the deer that roam my woods is anathema to me.

It just seems cruel and unfair, unless the deer has a gun and can shoot you back.

I knew my lack of enthusiasm would show through in my copy.

And when you don't write copy with enthusiasm, you're toast.

# CHAPTER 28

# Copy by the Numbers

### #1: Use specific numbers.

To quote Claude Hopkins from his classic book *Scientific Advertising*, "specifics sell."

Specifics make your writing stronger, more credible, more engaging, and improve its attention-getting power.

And use of numbers automatically adds specificity to your copy, making it stronger.

For instance, here is a benefit expressed in general terms: "Reduces energy consumption."

But it doesn't tell you whether the amount of energy savings is significant or trivial.

Adding a number makes it more specific: "Reduces energy consumption by 43%." And more meaningful.

### #2: Convey authority with numbers.

The British scientist Lord Kelvin once said: "When you can express something in numbers, then you know something about it."

Saying global warming is causing sea levels to rise forces the reader to guess how much the sea levels are rising.

Saying a NASA study forecasts those sea levels to rise one foot by 2050 comes across as more authoritative and credible.

"One foot" enables readers to gain a mental picture and visualize the magnitude and effect of those elevated water levels.

### #3: Add numerical parallelism.

Parallelism in writing occurs *when you repeat the same grammatical form in multiple parts of a sentence.*

*A classic example is this quotation from U.S. President John F. Kennedy:*

*"Ask not what your country can do for you; ask what you can do for your country.*

*Here's an example from a book title using the number two:*

*"How to Make Your Advertising Twice as Effective at Half the Cost."*

*This could also have been written as numerals to make the parallelism of the number 2 stand out even more:*

*"How to Make Your Advertising 2X as Effective at 1/2 the Cost."*

## #4: Numbers arouse curiosity.

Say your headline is "The 7 most common mistakes in retirement investing—and how to avoid them."

As an investor, you immediately make in your own mind a list of all the retirement investing mistakes you can think of.

If you come up with fewer than 7, you become curious to see which ones you may be missing.

If you come up with 7 or more, you want to know how their list matches up with your list—which of course may reveal something you have overlooked.

## #5: Write numbers in digits, not words.

Prefer numerals to numbers written out as words.

Therefore, write "26," not "twenty-six."

And write "5 ways" rather than "five ways."

## #6: Odd vs. even.

Prefer odd numbers because they make more of an impact on your readers than even numbers.

The proof? Testing; e.g., "5 reasons why" outperforms "4 reasons why."

## #7: Don't round off.

In many instances, even when you do not have an exact count, you can finagle your copy to deliberately use an odd number.

For instance, an article reported that when a huge aquarium in Berlin burst, "around 1,500 exotic fish" spilled out of the tank and onto the floor.

Now, you know that the tank owners did not have an exact count.

So I would have said that "1,507 exotic fish" were lost.

It sounds more accurate and real, and therefore is better at catching the reader's attention.

## #8: Making larger numbers seem even larger.

Numerals are generally preferable to writing numbers out in words.

But when the number is larger, writing out the word can in many cases more quickly convey the magnitude of size.

For instance, when that enormous aquarium in Berlin burst, it spilled 264,172 gallons of water.

I would have written it as "over a quarter of a million gallons."

Now, normally the rule is: the more specific the number, the better.

But whenever the numbers get into four figures or higher, consider writing out the number.

Because the words *thousand, million*, and *billion* trigger an instant mental impression that whatever it is, it's big.

Example: Even though "quarter of a million" is rounded off, to me it sounds bigger than 264,172.

## #9: Extend numbers to the right of the decimal point to make them seem bigger.

You can make any number seem larger by writing it out to the first or second decimal.

Instead, saying a stock returns a "78% gain," write the stock profit out to the second decimal; e.g., 78.54%.

Why? The reader's eye sees it as a 4-digit gain instead of a 2-digit gain, and so she mentally perceives 78.54% as much larger than 78%, even though in reality it is not.

## CHAPTER 29:

# The Motivating Sequence for Writing Kick-Butt Sales Letters

Can you write a kick-butt sales letter?

By that, I mean one that generates an avalanche of responses, leads, and orders?

One that, as my mentor, old-time direct mail copywriter Sig Rosenblum said, "Grabs the reader by the lapels and won't let go"?

There is a proven 5-step formula, used by Sig and many other top copywriters, for persuasive writing called the Motivating Sequence.

It has been proven to work for over a century—originally in direct mail, with billions of sales letters mailed.

And today, in the vast majority of marketing channels, media, and promotions. Especially in both emails and landers.

Here are the 5 steps of the Motivating Sequence:

### 1: Get attention.

Unless you can get your prospects to stop trashing, turning the page, bypassing, deleting, or clicking away from your sales copy, you have lost them before you have even gotten started.

In copy, the headline has the main job of getting attention. Here is a "swipe file" of headlines that have been proven to engage prospects, boosting both readership and response:

https://www.bly.com/newsite/Pages/DMNCOL19.htm

### 2: Identify the prospect's problem.

In your lead, start by stating the main problem the prospect has that your product can solve.

For instance, a letter selling a water filtration technology to municipal engineers responsible for treating water or wastewater streams began:

*Do you have a potable water supply or waste stream that contains organic contaminants?*

*And have you considered activated carbon as the ideal treatment, only to ultimately reject deep-bed activated carbon installations because of the cost?*

### 3: Position your product as the solution.

Often this can be done in a quick transition—sometimes just a few sentences:

*Ecosorb filter precoats may be the answer for you. These patented, carbon-containing precoats can be utilized at reasonable cost for cleanup of contaminated water.*

### 4: Prove your claim.

Present facts, features, statistics, test results, studies, endorsements, testimonials, operating principles, technical specifications, data, and other information that convinces prospects your claim is true.

The Ecosorb letter explains that the superior performance was due to a unique technology in which discrete particles of activated carbon are attached to filter fibers. Other advantages included porous structure, large exposed surface area, and high adsorption capacity.

### 5: Ask for action.

In direct selling, this usually means filling in an order form and making payment.

In lead generation, we generally have two offers.

The "hard offer" requires direct action. From Ecosorb: "We'd be delighted to evaluate a water sample to see if Ecosorb can handle your particular requirements."

The "soft offer" requires less action and commitment, which in the Ecosorb letter was the offer of a free technical report.

The Motivating Sequence then is:

1: Get attention.

2: State the problem.

3: Position your product as the solution.

4: Prove that your product is the best solution.

5: Ask for an order or inquiry.

Using the Motivating Sequence to generate leads, the Ecosorb letter produced an 11% response.

# CHAPTER 30

# Five Perspectives on the Copywriter/Client Relationship

Just as different copywriters have different attitudes toward their clients, so too clients have differing attitudes about copywriters.

For the copywriters, their relationships with clients fall into one of these five categories:

## #1: Vendor.

A vendor is the lowest level.

It implies the copywriter simply does whatever the client tells him.

The client is always right, and he is also paying the bills.

So the copywriter is at all times subservient to and beneath the client.

I often see this subservience in both newbie copywriters and small agencies.

They follow all client commands without questioning or challenging the client—even if they think the client is wrong or there is a better approach that could make the ad stronger.

There are two reasons for this subservience. For newbie copywriters, it is often a lack of confidence in their knowledge and abilities.

For some small agencies, it is sometimes because they desperately need the work, and are afraid that if they express a contrary opinion, they might be fired.

## #2: Adversarial.

Some people, both on the client side and the agency side, are naturally contentious and just love to argue—especially when clients want to change their copy.

About this, my colleague, Cam Foote, said the following:

"The first draft is your recommendation. If the client wants to change or reject it, explain why you think it works. If after that, the client remains adamant about the copy changes, acquiesce pleasantly."

### #3: Arrogant superiority.

I recently met a copywriter who said his clients never changed a word of his copy—because he explicitly told them not to "interfere" with his genius by suggesting edits.

He said the reason was: "I simply know what I am doing. And the client doesn't."

To me, this is both arrogance of the highest order—and also just plain wrong.

Yes, you as a copywriter, of course, know copy.

But many clients know their products, technology, and markets far better than you do.

And some my clients are even great copywriters in their own right.

So to dismiss the value they bring to the table … or claim you as the copywriter are well-nigh omnipotent … is stupid, plain and simple.

### #4: Collaborator.

Once, a long time ago, I used to buy into the premise of copywriter as the ultimate master of persuasion.

I told clients that copywriting is not a group sport.

And when they hired me to write their copy, I advised that for best results, there should only be one cook in the kitchen. Me.

But as the years went by, I saw the value in making copywriting more of a collaborative process.

Especially when the client:

… is very smart.

… knows marketing.

… is an idea person.

… has superior knowledge of prior copy tests and their results.

… knows his industry or niche inside and out.

... is a good writer.

... or even a very good copywriter.

## #5: Advisor.

A copywriter who "only" writes copy does as the client requests.

For instance, the client wants a postcard—and so the copywriter writes a postcard.

Sensible enough. And reasonable.

But as an advisor—or "marketing consultant"—the copywriter might start more strategically, exploring with the client....

... is a postcard the best format for the mailing?

... what about a sales letter in a #10 envelope?

... or a tri-fold self-mailer?

... should it be a single mailing—or a series?

... direct mail only—or integrated with digital?

... follow-up with responders and non-responders.

... offer and price testing.

... and other important issues.

Many top copywriters and their clients agree that a copywriter who is both a copywriter and an advisor can often deliver superior value and results to her clients.

# CHAPTER 31

# Avoid These Common B2B Copy Mistakes

Whether your B2B copy is written by ad agencies or in-house, beware of these 5 frequent copywriting mistakes:

### #1: Assuming your copy is too boring.

Many lay people who write or read B2B documents worry that their copy is boring.

But "boring" to whom?

People outside a given industry may indeed find the copy a snooze—to them.

But you are not writing B2B copy for you; you are writing it for prospects.

And, though not of great interest to you, the information may be engaging—even useful and important—to potential customers.

In which case it may be very good copy indeed.

### #2: Cutting copy indiscriminately.

In their classic book, *The Elements of Writing*, Strunk and White say good writing is concise.

But "concise" and "short" are two different things.

"Short" is a synonym for brief.

"Concise" is not.

Concise means that you get your message across to the reader *in the fewest words possible.*

When the copy seems too long, do not make the mistake of simply editing out parts you find too boring or do not understand—as some marketing professional do.

You must go through it and thoughtfully remove unnecessary text, which may include redundant words and phrases or long-winded copy, without inadvertently cutting essential information.

### #3: Overuse of jargon.

Don't confuse technical terminology with jargon.

Technical terms are precise language to describe a technical thing or topic.

Example: "Operating system" is a legitimate technical term, because it is well understood, specific, and there is no plainer way to say it.

Jargon is language more complex than the ideas it serves to communicate.

For instance, "deplane" is airline jargon you should avoid.

Instead, just say "get off the plane."

If you are a techie communicating with other techies, using jargon judiciously can help show your readers that you are one of them.

And people universally like to buy from people who are like them.

But overuse of jargon can make it seem like you are writing to impress—not express.

Also, jargon risks poor communication with readers who don't know all your lingo.

### #4: Failure to spell out abbreviations and acronyms.

Abbreviations and acronyms should be spelled out the first time you use them—for instance, "VTOL (vertical take-off and landing)."

The exceptions are abbreviations (e.g., DNA) and acronyms (laser) with which your readers are already familiar.

### #5: Irrelevant copy and content.

According to an article in *ANA Business Marketing SmartBrief*, nearly 8 out of 10 B2B buyers say vendors are serving them irrelevant content.

Example: a product brochure selling a company's lithium battery began with a detailed discussion of lithium.

Interesting? Well, yes, at least to me as a lay reader.

But the prospect, who is an automotive engineer, has a more immediate and urgent need to know why he should specify this company's lithium battery over others.

# CHAPTER 32

# The Powerful 4 P's Copywriting Formula

Years ago, I discovered the 4 P's formula while writing copy for numerous dietary supplements, for which the formula fit like a glove.

But then, I quickly found that the 4 P's formula works like gangbusters across a wide spectrum of niches—everything from investments and high-tech, to home improvement and insurance. The 4 P's are: pain, promise, proof, and push:

- ***The first step is to name and magnify your prospect's PAIN.***

  The pain may be SYMPTOMATIC. Meaning the prospect is aware of it; e.g., money worries, ill health, leaky roof, kids failing school, difficulty hearing, blurry vision.

  Or, the pain may be ASYMPTOMATIC, meaning the prospect is not aware of the problem yet; e.g., termite rot in your house with no visible evidence of termites or damaged wood.

  When the pain is asymptomatic, your copy must begin by first convincing the prospect that he may have the problem, and should therefore take steps to eliminate the problem before it gets worse.

- ***The second of the 4 P's is PROMISE.*** Your product must promise the reader that it can and most likely will solve his problem.

  If the problem is SYMPTOMATIC, the promise is that the product will eliminate the problem and all of its symptoms and ill effects.

  If the problem is ASYMPTOMATIC, the promise is that either the product will prevent the problem from ever happening in the first place.

  Or, if the problem is present, the product will slow, halt, and then reverse the condition until it is gone.

- *The third step is PROOF.* You must provide evidence to convince the prospect that your promise is true, and your product will deliver on it.

  Just some of the types of proof include: testimonials ... client list ... track record ... technical and design features ... demonstrations ... guarantees ... laboratory tests ... press coverage ... reviews ... size ... power ... reliability ... and many more.

- *The fourth and final of the 4 P's is PUSH*, which means getting the prospect to buy.

  PUSH is the job of the offer. An "offer" is what you will give the prospect when he responds, as well as what he has to do to get it, including the payment and terms of purchase.

  There are many different offers; the one used to depend on the product, prospects, price point, and medium:

- Emails used to generate leads for enterprise software tell you to click on a hyperlink in the email to download a free white paper.

- TV commercials for insurance instruct you to call a toll-free number—usually to get an information kit, a premium (free gift), and possibly a rate quote.

- Direct mail packages encourage you to order by completing and mailing a reply card, scanning a Quick Response Code, or visiting a specific URL.

CHAPTER 33:

# Creativity in Advertising

Creativity, when used to achieve your communication objective, can often enhance copy and content.

But there are 5 factors in creating great copy and content that are even more important than creativity:

## #1: The "big idea."

The big idea is the central premise around which your ad is based.

People argue, and perhaps rightly so, that there is nothing new under the sun.

The solution?

You have to say the same old thing—but in a new, fresh, and compelling way.

For instance, all weight loss products make similar claims along the lines of "lose X many pounds in Y weeks."

An ad for a diet shake had this headline: "Drink yourself thin!"

It worked because, even though it is essentially the same old claim—the product can help you lose weight—it says so in a way prospects hadn't quite heard before.

Namely, that you can lose weight without exercise, pills, or starvation diets—just by slaking your thirst with a tasty drink.

## #2: An attention-grabbing hook or twist.

Here again, you may be saying something old, but the trick is to get the reader's attention by giving it a fresh spin.

For instance, when promoting microcap stocks, the message is always the same: "Buy this stock now and make money when it goes up in price."

For a promotion on a small online gaming company stock, the copywriter discovered that the company earned revenue every time any customers place a bet on the site, regardless of whether the customer wins.

Based on this, he wrote a successful promo with this headline: "Get Paid to Gamble."

### #3: Engaging stories.

Stories work well because we all like stories.

Good *personal* stories, when well crafted, work even better.

Because they are yours and yours alone.

And because you can write them in the first person.

Example from a successful direct mail package selling a health newsletter:

"When I was 16, my father died of a heart attack."

By the way, when I asked ChatGPT whether AI can replace human content writers and copywriters, the software replied:

"As an AI language model, I do not have the ability to use personal experiences to inform my writing, or capture the nuances of human emotion, in the same way a human writer can."

### #4: Emotion.

People are driven to purchase by emotional appeals, and we then justify our spending with rational arguments.

A classic example is the ad campaign for Carters sleep wear:

"If they Could Just Stay Little Till Their Carters Wear Out," which tapped into the intense love a parent feels for her child—as in this Carter's TV commercial:

### #5: A clearly differentiating unique selling proposition (USP).

The USP says what makes your product different and better than all other products in its category.

Also called the "value proposition," it is the compelling reason why the consumer should buy your product instead of your competitor's product.

A good example from back in the day, when I was a kid, is Wonder Bread.

White bread has little nutritional value, so to convince moms to give it to their kids, Wonder Bread added what were arguably small amount of a dozen vitamins and minerals to the product.

They then positioned Wonder Bread as the most nutritional white bread with this specific and evidence-based claim and USP:

"Only Wonder Bread Helps Build Strong Bodies 12 Ways."

Other classic USPs:

- "Burger King—Have It Your Way"—Making a successful USP out of the (to me) rather mundane advantage that you can specify what you want and don't want on your Whopper.
- "M&M's Melt in Your Mouth, Not in Your Hands"—Their innovation of a hard candy shell for M&M's eliminated getting chocolate all over your fingers and face.
- "Mr. Bubble Gets You Bubbly Clean"—A children's bath soap that bubbled in the bathtub that was so  much fun the kids were eager for bath time ... invented by a friend of my late father.

# CHAPTER 34

# Tips for Writing Profitable Financial Copy

**#1:** ***Offer the reader new ideas.*** A financial consulting firm helps high-net worth clients lower their taxes—by helping these families establish their own private charitable foundation.

Copy begins with the headline, "New FREE Special Report Reveals Little-Known Strategy Millionaires Use to Keep Their Wealth in Their Hands—and Out of Uncle Sam's." The headline builds curiosity by not revealing *what* this tax-saving strategy is. The prospect must read the copy to find out. And send for the report to get the important details.

**#2:** ***Create a sense of immediacy or urgency.*** At times when interest rates drop precipitously, a bank sends out mailings encouraging customers to take advantage of the favorable low rates. The envelope teaser: "4 reasons why there has never been a better time than NOW to get a home equity loan from ABC Bank."

**#3:** ***Highlight the offer.*** The envelope teaser for a mailing promoting a bank card for businesses reads, in large bold type, "Earn $750 Bonus Cash Back." Also offered in the sales letter inside are no annual fee, extra cards for employees at no additional cost, 1.5% cash back on every business purchase, protection against unauthorized charges, and introductory 0% APR for the first 12 months.

**#4:** ***Stress low cost and money savings.*** A letter from an association offering term life insurance says, "At your current age of 63, it costs as little as 79 cents a day to leave your family $10,000 in cash. That's less than a cup of coffee."

**#5:** ***Reward your preferred customers.*** The call-to-action (CTA) in a mailer promoting auto insurance targets drivers with clean records, who can often qualify for a lower rate: "Good drivers deserve a good fit. If you're looking for customized coverage at a great price, call us today."

*6: **Help your prospects avoid financial hardships.*** My father, an insurance agent, drummed into me the danger of not having adequate insurance coverage—a mistake made by millions of Americans. A letter from a health care insurance carrier drives home this point: "When you're uninsured or under-insured, illness or injury might means thousands of dollars in medical expenses—hefty doctor and hospital bills you have to pay out of your own pocket."

*7: **Use "visceral" language.*** That means slang or other expressions and phrases conveying more emotion and drama than dull, straightforward financial writing. A letter offering consumers a line of credit starts with this: "Are you sick and tired of shelling out big money to pay off high-interest loans and credit account bills each month?"

*8: **Questions.*** In your copy, ask a question. It should be a question that the reader does not know the answer to—an answer he would be highly motivated and even eager to find out. A letter promoting homeowner's insurance for antique houses has this headline: "What will you do when your homeowner's insurance refuses to pay for the full cost of restoring your home to pristine condition?"

*9: **Write copy that targets your ideal customer with laser focus.*** The trick here is to use copy that is so specific about who the ideal customer for this offer would be, that when the customer reads it, he is instantly convinced that the offer is tailor made for him—just what he wants and needs. The headline on a postcard from a property tax reduction service reads:

"PROPERTY TAX BILLING NOTICE for owners and tenants of land and buildings in Sarasota County, Florida."

*10: **Forecasts and predictions.*** The public has been trained to watch and accept predictions, projections, pronouncements, outlooks, forecasts, and even "guesstimates" from investment "gurus" pontificating on TV and online. The editors for an investment advisory service on energy stocks made this bold prediction that oil prices were going to rise: "$100 a barrel crude oil. It can make you rich. Or it can make you poor."

# CHAPTER 35

# Ten Quick and Easy Ways to Establish Credibility in Your Copy

**#1**: *Align yourself with a well-known and respected brand.* An investment advisor in Canada, for example, is also a vice president to a major Canadian bank. Many investors prefer Vanguard to funds they have never heard of.

**#2**: *Show your recent successes.* Real estate agents, for instance, let prospects know that the agent is in the million-dollar club. Or they highlight recent sales of homes in the area.

**#3**: *Track record.* Track record is your performance either since inception or over a specific period of time. Track record can show high returns of individual investment or compare annual gains to the S&P 500 or other benchmarks. For an accounting service, it might be percentage of clients getting a tax refund.

**#4**: *Credentials.* These include licenses, certifications, awards, honors, training, college, degrees, and other evidence of how qualified, knowledgeable, and expert you are.

**#5**: *Let them know you act as a fiduciary.* Always act in the investor's best interests and not in your own. Marketing and sales promotions should say that this is how you operate, and if possible, give examples.

**#6**: *Community.* Because so many financial services firms serve clients within the same geographic area, supporting the local community builds goodwill and makes people like you more. And doing good works always raises your star.

**#7**: *Unique methodology.* By offering a smart investment methodology or special financial instrument many people don't know about (e.g., private lender mortgage notes, closed-end mutual funds), or a strategy that seems different and innovative, you demonstrate that you know something that your competition seems not to. And all else being equal, people prefer doing business with an expert.

**#8: *Media proof.*** By media proof, we mean being covered, in a positive way, by the mainstream media (e.g., TV, radio, newspapers) as well as digital media (e.g., e-newsletters, blogs, websites).

**#9: *Social proof.*** Social proof means demonstrating that people think highly of you. This can be anything from you being the biggest bank in the country, to getting 5-star online reviews, to being praised by influential bloggers

**#10: *Testimonials and endorsements.*** Testimonials are favorable comments about you from your clients. Endorsements are favorable comments from industry associations and your industry peers. Suggestion: Say what the endorser's key financial credential or fame is. Reason: Though you may think everyone knows who the endorser is, often many people do not.

CHAPTER 36:

# Marketing to Techies

As a chemical engineer, I've spent a lot of time hanging out with, observing, listening to, and working fellow engineers. And I've been writing B2B copy for decades. Based on this experience, here's what I've observed about marketing B2B products and services to engineers, scientists, IT professionals, programmers, and other techies:

**#1:** A lot of techies snub and look down their noses at non-techies. In college, these non-techies are likely to be liberal arts majors. In the business world, they often include marketing and sales professionals.

**#2:** Many engineers see their work as more difficult, and therefore requiring greater intelligence, than marketing, sales, or management. As a result, techies may feel they are smarter than marketers.

**#3:** Engineers often assume that both senior management and marketing staff know little or nothing about industrial equipment, or its basic technology and operating principles. For this reason, they may be highly skeptical of the content and copy you or company puts out.

**#4:** Engineers also look down their noses at marketing. They see it as an unwholesome mental chore and a distasteful practice. So to them, marketing content is far less credible than purely "technical" information—the kind of data they might hear, for instance, at a presentation by an engineer speaking at a meeting of their professional association.

**#5:** The more promotional, hyped-up, and like a consumer ad your B2B copy sounds, the more likely engineers are to reject it out of hand, based simply on the negative perception that you are making a "sales pitch" rather than delivering useful technical content.

**#6:** Engineers believe that websites and other marketing channels for industrial equipment should focus strongly on features and specifications. And that most other content—including branding, messaging, value proposition, and USP—are unnecessary, extraneous, and a waste of their time.

**#7:** Technical buyers operate under the delusion that they make purchase decisions only with their logical minds, based on evaluation of facts, graphs, charts, diagrams, and numbers. They either are highly skeptical—or else totally disbelieve—that an engineer or technician could possibly be influenced by emotional appeals.

**#8:** Writing style and word choice are of two sides of the B2B copywriting coin. On the one hand, technical buyers understand technical terminology. And when we use it to communicate with them, they feel as if our copy is speaking to them peer-to-peer. That helps boost our selling power, because people prefer buying from people they like. And people generally prefer people who are like them.

**#9:** On the other hand, all copy—both B2B and B2C—should be clear, crisp, and concise. It should be technical enough to inform and persuade the most knowledgeable experts. But also easily understood by all your prospects, even the less experienced. In 4 years of writing for industry, I have never heard someone say about my B2B copy, "This is too easy to read."

**#10:** Engineers especially are visually oriented. So if you are writing about a process, be sure to include a process diagram. Explaining a procedure? Show a flow chart. Talking about your pelletizing machine? Show the pellets.

**#11:** If you need to present multiple pieces of data, put them in a table. Engineers believe the British scientist Lord Kelvin, who said, "When you can measure something, and express it in numbers, then you know something about it."

**#12:** A rule of writing popular science for the general public is that for each equation you include in your article, you will lose 10% of your readership. But engineers and scientists like equations. Mathematics is a familiar language for them. So marketing writers should embrace math, not shy away from it.

# CHAPTER 37

# The 3 Keys to a Winning Unique Selling Proposition

There are two problems marketers have today when it comes to formulating a winning Unique Selling Proposition or "USP."

The first is that most are unaware of the original 3-part definition of USP, as formulated by Rosser Reeves in his 1961 book *Reality in Advertising.*

The core of the USP, as stated by Reeves, is that "each advertisement must make a proposition to the consumer." And this proposition must meet three criteria for it to make your marketing stronger.

First, it must say to the reader, "Buy this product and you will get this specific benefit."

Second, it must be unique—a claim that the competition either cannot or does not offer.

Third, it must be so strong that it can pull over new customers to your product.

You have to know and deliberately implement all three criteria to formulate a truly powerful USP.

When you ask someone what a USP is, almost everyone knows the answer.

But then ask them "What are the 3 components needed for a winning USP?"

Not one marketer in a hundred knows. And not knowing what makes a USP great is a major impediment to formulating a winning one.

The second problem with USP as it specifically applies to B2B is with the third criteria: making it so strong that it pulls over new customers to your product.

The most common USP mistake in B2B marketing, most notably among companies that sell complex (e.g., fluid dispensing machines) vs. simple (e.g., paper cups) products is, well, a bit of a "cheat"— as follows.

To formulate a selling proposition that is unique, many industrial marketers often take the lazy way out. How? By achieving that differentiation with a feature that is trivial—rather than one that is important and actually meaningful to the buyer.

For instance, one manufacturer of gears had this USP: they reduced friction in machine operation by using ball bearings made out of smooth, low-friction plastic instead of metal.

But "plastic" vs. metal ball bearings, or "low-friction" vs. conventional ball bearings, did little to move the sales needle.

However, it turned out that, with the lower friction came a number of other advantages. Including less machine wear. Greater reliability. Longer-lasting parts. And no need to keep the bearings lubricated with grease.

And guess what? The winning USP turned out to be "greaseless ball bearings."

Why? It was easy to remember. Distinctive. And most important, *it delivered a major and significant advantage to the user by eliminating the costly and labor-intensive relubrication of bearings.* So "greaseless" was the product advantage wording the market responded to best. Not just "plastic" or "low friction."

Now, with its greaseless bearings, the gear manufacturer had all 3 criteria of a winning USP: a powerful benefit, a clear difference, and a way to communicate to the buyer that this difference was an important advantage, and not just a trivial design factor—as is so often the case in industrial products.

# CHAPTER 38

# Is Jargon Always Bad?

The other day, I received a postcard from the local Acme supermarket where we buy our groceries.

In one bullet point, the copy says the meat counter is a superior value. One reason cited is that Acme has "butchers who trim, bone, spatchcock, and grind to order."

Now, I must admit, if I was the copywriter writing that copy, it would never have been occurred to me to use the "spatchcock."

If the audience for the postcard was chefs, butchers, gourmets, or meat connoisseurs, the supermarket copywriter might get away with this.

However, the postcard mailing targeted all of the store's customers, and was not aimed specifically at either food professionals or even foodies.

Specifically, the piece was mailed to households located near the store: Our neighbors and fellow Acme shoppers who are, like us, every day folk. Not Gordon Ramsey.

And I suspected that, when I am grocery shopping at our Acme, not one customer in 100 knows what spatchcock is.

So, in my impromptu and statistically invalid in-store survey, I stood at the meat counter, held up the postcard, and asked about a dozen of my fellow shoppers if they knew what a "spatchcock" is.

Admittedly, though the survey results may have been influenced by bias confirmation, the fact remains that *not a single person* I asked had any idea of what "spatchcock" mean.

And, although the postcard was B2C, the matter of word choice—and in particular the decision to use jargon and technical terms—is an even a bigger and more frequent issue in B2B copywriting.

To tackle it clearly, first we have to determine whether any given word or phrase is in  jargon vs. legitimate technical terminology.

So what's the difference?

Sociologist Susan K. Brownmiller defines jargon as "language more complex than the ideas it serves to communicate."

Applying that criterion, "operating system" is correct use of technical language, and not jargon, because it is the most accurate—and the most direct—way to refer to MS-DOS, Linux, and other operating system code.

On the other hand, "deplane" *is* jargon, because even though it's short and sweet, there is a better way to say it using plain, simple English: "get off the plane."

When writing to a lay audience (e.g., people who are not specialists), say things as plainly and simply as you can, whenever possible.

However, if the use of a technical term seems the clearest and most direct way of communicating your idea to the lay audience, then be sure to at least define the term the first time you use it in your copy or content.

As for overly complex language, in *The Elements of Writing,* Strunk and White advise: "Avoid needless jargon."

For instance, an ad for a material conveying system told the reader that the processed material was "gravimetrically conveyed" from the machine to a waiting storage silo. Well, why not just say "dumped?"

Similarly, an ad for a dental splint said the device "stabilizes mobile dentition." Instead,  just say the product "keeps loose teeth in place." In the same vein, do not write "utilize" when you can  just as easily say "use."

Why do I believe I am right? Because, after having written thousands of promotions, not a single prospect or reader has ever complained that my copy was too easy to read.

# CHAPTER 39

# How to Write and Design a "Prospect-Qualifying" Landing Page

There are two basic approaches to creating B2B content download pages, and whenever you use either one of them, you are leaving money on the table.

The first type is the *quick download page*. This simple page requires only that the prospect enters his name and email address. Nothing else. In exchange, he can immediately download a free white paper PDF or other lead magnet.

On the plus side, because it's so easy to use, quick download pages have high conversion rates. On the minus side, because the only thing you know about the prospect is name and email address, it is merely an inquiry, and not a qualified lead.

The second type is the *data-collection download page*. These pages gather a lot of information about the prospects, allowing you to better qualify the inquiries. The drawback is fewer responses. Reason: as a rule of thumb, for each additional field you force prospects to submit, the conversion rate declines by approximately 10 percent.

I recommend a third approach, which I call the *prospect-qualifying download page*. The key is that this landing page performs *two* functions. It increases conversion rates with prominent lead magnet offers, and it also qualifies the prospect by simply requiring him to check a box gauging his level of interest. So, it is quick and easy to complete and submit while retaining high conversion rate.

Here is one of my own prospect-qualifying download pages offering a free special report, *The B2B Marketing Handbook.* This PDF is a compilation of a couple of dozen of my articles on various B2B marketing topics:

https://www.bly.com/b2bhandbook/

Go online and click on it now to see the approach in action. The left side of the page "sells" the prospects on the lead magnet, with a strong call-to-action headline, and bullet points teasing information in the handbook the reader may be interested in.

On the right side there is a narrow column. It collects some information about the prospect. But more important, the prospect can check any or all of three different boxes to instantly communicate what he wants from you, as follows:

#1: "Send me your free lead magnet."

#2: "Send me more information on your product or service."

#3: "Call me so I can discuss my needs and get a no-risk price quote or estimate for the product or service I may want to purchase."

How this qualifies the inquires is simple:

* People who check only box #1 and just request your freebie are either marginally qualified or not at all qualified.

   Why do I say only "marginally qualified?" It's based on an assumption that a person would not request your lead magnet on topic X unless solving a problem related to topic X was one of his concerns. However, I say "marginally," because you will get some inquiries from people who just like to get free stuff. (Back in the day, we called them "brochure collectors.)

* People who check box #2 are more qualified, because they specifically want to get more details on, and possibly get a quote or cost estimate for, your product or service.

* People who check box #3 are the most qualified leads, for two reasons. First, they are willing to talk with you. And second, a prospect who wants a price quote is most likely farther down your sales funnel, and therefore easier to close.

In short, *the prospect-qualifying download page* gives you the best of both worlds: more total leads as well as a greater number of qualified leads. In other words, that rarest of marketing result: quantity plus quality. In B2B, it doesn't get much better than that, right?

# CHAPTER 40:

# Writing High-Conversion Call-to-Action Buttons

Offering a lead magnet is perhaps the most common call-to-action (CTA) for lead generation. And the click button or link often and straightforwardly reads "Click here now."

Although lead magnets can vary greatly in format, medium, length, and content, one of the most common and popular offers is the download of a free PDF, such as an ebook, special report, or white paper.

The actual download is achieved by the prospect clicking on a button on a landing page or in an email.

As for the CTA, there are a few different of words you can use in your copy when you want prospects to respond to your free content offers.

But when writing your copy, you should be aware that they have slightly different connotations:

- **Access ...** makes the content sounds exclusive and valuable. Also sounds a bit technical, leading edge, important, and confidential. "Access" is a word that grabs your attention and makes you feel like getting the lead magnet is somewhat of a privilege. Or that the content may even at times be kept secure and restricted.

- **Get ...** straightforward, simple, and direct. People like to get stuff and be given stuff. This short imperative appeals to the prospect's desire to *get* something.

- **Claim ...** makes the prospect think he has hit gold with your content offer. Gold miners famously "staked" claims for potential mineral reserves and deposits. In a lottery, winners claim their prize. In a casino, gamblers claim their winnings. It sounds as if the prospect is being given an exciting opportunity to get something of real value.

- **Download ...** a computer-age term that emphasizes the speed and ease of getting the lead magnet. The appeal here is that getting the requested content is quick and simple. Much faster than direct mail where you have to complete a reply element, mail it back to the advertiser, and then wait for the requested material to arrive back to you by post.

- **Read ...** a bit dull and sounds like work. If you use "read" in your CTA and offer, add copy that makes it sound like it's not a lot of time and effort; e.g., "Reading Time: Just 7 Minutes."

- **Request ...** reasonable language, but it may connote that the prospect is a supplicant of sorts. Might sound to the prospect as if he is in the position of begging you for a favor—and may or may not in fact be given the lead magnet.

- **Let's talk ...** a friendly, informal way of inviting the prospect to call you to continue the conversation.

A radio commercial for a vocabulary course said, "People judge you by the words you use." And your prospects judge you by the words you use in your copy.

As suggested here, the tone and intention of your CTA varies with the imperative verb you choose. Yes, it's only one word. But the word you use can affect your prospect's emotions and actions more than you might think.

# CHAPTER 41

# A Common Misconception About "Boring" B2B Copy

A recent article in *ANA Business Marketing SmartBrief* (3/11/22) promulgates the old saw that B2B copy is boring.

The author, a Madison Avenue creative director, says an important step in eliminating the "B-to-Boring" stereotype is to "earn the attention of audiences by creating interesting content."

But, I ask…interesting to whom?

The reason so many advertising types say B2B is "boring" and dull is that they find the subject matter boring.

And it is—to them—because they are not the target audience for the ad.

They are not the prospects for the product being advertised, so it is of no interest to them.

And frequently, they don't understand the product or the problem it solves at all.

But it doesn't matter that the copy is boring to them and their fellow ad agency compatriots.

What matters is that, in a successful B2B ad, the copy is NOT boring to the intended audience.

Rather, that it is interesting to the reader.

And readers of B2B copy are often not the same as lay folks.

They often have specialized knowledge based on education or their work, or both. And they need to buy things for their work a lay reader does not need.

The success of their business, and their success on the job, frequently depends on buying the product that is best for a particular application.

Which makes B2B buying a "considered purchase." Something they really must think through carefully.

This is in sharp contrast to many consumer purchases—such as fast food, shampoo, other low-priced items that are "impulse buys."

For instance, my friend JA, who ran a successful industrial ad agency in Michigan, had a client that made acid-resistant bricks.

The bricks were used to line metal process vessels that held sulfuric acid. Without the brick lining, the acid eats away at the metal tank containing it.

The prospects for the bricks were virtually all engineers and plant managers, and the latter all had an engineering degree.

So JA created an ad that outperformed all previous ads the company had run for the product.

The headline: "Handling Sulfuric Acid."

You may find that exceedingly dull, pedantic, and totally lacking in emotional appeal.

But engineers in sulfuric acid plants responded in droves, because it identified and promised a solution to one of their most pressing problems: storing a strong acid safely.

Also, the headline implied that the engineer would learn something just by reading the ad, whether he bought the product or not. "Handling Sulfuric Acid" feels like content marketing, not sales copy.

Some of JA's colleagues in other ad agencies said that the ad—especially the headline—was indeed "boring."

But, you must always ask in creating B2B advertising ... boring to whom? To you? Or to the reader?

# CHAPTER 42:

# Avoid "Google Goulash"

In an email (4/29/22), Createxdigital offered a simple yet powerful research suggestion for content marketing.

Specifically, they advised content writers to actually *talk to prospects and customers*—both directly in interviews, and also indirectly by "listening in" on sales calls. Their email message instructed:

"Interview existing customers to find out what challenges they hit in their jobs and why they use your product. Makes notes of 'friction points.' [Also] be a silent observer on sales calls and make notes of [those] friction points."

While the idea of picking up the phone and calling people might strike some of today's content writers and copywriters as a radical notion, it is not. In fact, doing this kind of proactive, primary research is how traditional journalists have been writing their articles for years.

Why? Because primary research enables you to have discussions with subject matter experts and others who know more about your topic than you do.

As a result, you gather information that is more detailed, specific, insightful, in-depth, expert, accurate, and often much more interesting than you otherwise would.

To my mind, too many content writers today are either lazy about doing the hard work of primary research—or indifferent about the quality of their finished product.

So they never pick up the phone or send an email to a source in search of information, and instead take the easy way out: They Google the subject matter. Grab the first 3 or 4 articles they find with their online search. And then cobble these old articles together into their current article.

They mistakenly believe their new article is indeed "new." But actually, their piece is just a warmed-over rehash of what has already been written about that same topic before—an endless number of times.

The end result is "Google goulash."

Now, Google goulash is quick and easy to produce. And therefore, dirt-cheap to commission and buy. ChatGPT produces a lot of Google goulash.

But unlike mainstream journalism, Google goulash has little to offer the reader in the way of originality, freshness, intelligence, or genuine value of any kind.

Hint: If the writer's only mission was to improve SEO for the marketer, the articles she writes—more likely than not—will be cut-rate content: utter Google goulash.

Google goulash rarely, if ever, positions you as an authoritative expert. It does not support your brand. It does not engage your audience. In fact, it often does the opposite.

Worse, if your Google goulash-writer copies or plagiarizes too much text from the source articles, Google may detect the duplication, and then penalize you in the search engine rankings when you post your new article on your site.

Obviously, not what you want, right?

# CHAPTER 43

# Six Keys to Writing B2B Copy That Works

B2B marketing can fail when your copywriter doesn't understand the 6 things he needs to know to write the strongest copy:

### #1: The audience.

In B2B, the people creating the ads are often not members of the target market.

Therefore, the more specialized the audience you target, the more likely it is that some members of your marketing team have a less than solid—and possibly even weak—understanding of your prospects.

In particular: who they are ... what they believe ... what they desire ... and what their emotional makeup and core feelings.

Also: their level of technical expertise, job responsibilities, and technology preferences and prejudices.

### #2: The problem your product solves for the buyer.

Accurately identifying the big problem your product solves for the buyer is critical to engaging them on both an emotional as well as a logical level.

For instance, a mailer for AARP Medicare Supplement Insurance Plans leads with a clear, specific, and immediate problem statement the recipients can relate to:

> *Original Medicare only covers about 80% of Part B medical costs. So, if you're 65 years old and enrolled in Original Medicare, you may not be totally covered.*

### #3: You don't understand the product.

This is often the case when the marketing team either has little or no technical background, or else may lack familiarity with the specific product or its applications.

### #4: You are not familiar with competitive products and alternatives solutions.

For instance, you may be familiar with the trays your company manufactures for refinery distillation towers that separate crude into gasoline, diesel, heating oil, and other hydrocarbons.

But you may not understand how other types of tower internals—such as random packing, saddles, and rings— work … and the advantages of trays over these alternatives.

Can you clearly articulate the value proposition and unique selling proposition of your product vs. others? If not, you are at a disadvantage in trying to convince prospects that your solution is different and better.

### #5: You don't possess enough facts to prove your case.

You have to dig deep. Reason: B2B buyers who are technical or from a niche industry know a lot about applications and equipment. And their success on the job depends in part on making the right purchase decisions.

So they know what they are looking for. The more proof you have that your product has superior performance, the more persuasive your copy will be.

Examples of proof include:
- Charts and graphs.
- Field performance.
- Third party testing.
- Case studies.
- Specifications.
- Operating principles.

In addition, if you don't know what you are talking about, and are faking your way through it, prospects will spot it. Your copy won't ring true. And your credibility will evaporate.

## #6: You don't have a clear and specific call to action (CTA).

- A strong CTA tells readers:
- What they get when they respond.
- What they have to do to get it.
- Why they should want it.
- Why they should respond now instead of later.

The Medicare insurance mailer mentioned earlier has the following CTA covering 3 types of information potential insurance buyers may be seeking:

*To learn more about AARP Medicare Supplement Insurance Plans.*
*In just one phone call, a licensed insurance agent may:*
- *Walk you through your options.*
- *Answer your questions.*
- *Enroll you over the phone.*

Makes sense, right? When you are shopping for insurance, you want to know your coverage options, terms, premiums, rating of insurance carrier, and how to enroll.

# CHAPTER 44:

# Editorial-Style
# "Implied Content"

"Editorial-style implied content" is an under-publicized—yet extremely potent—copywriting technique with 2 essential characteristics:

First, "editorial-style" means the ad looks and reads more like an article than an advertisement.

Second, "implied content" means the headline promises useful information.

A classic consumer example is a magazine ad that Duncan-Hines ran years ago:

"The Secret to Moisture, Richer Chocolate Cake."

"Secret" is a powerful selling word for "editorial-style implied content," because people want to know what the secret is.

It sounds like you are going to get a recipe for great chocolate cake—one that your friends and neighbors may not know.

You do—but the "recipe" is to use Duncan-Hines Chocolate Cake Mix.

So the ad accomplishes two things.

First, it delivers on its promise of showing you how to make a great chocolate cake.

Second, it drives sales of the product, because Duncan-Hines Chocolate Cake Mix is the key ingredient; others include eggs, butter, and milk.

Now let's look at a B2B sample of "editorial-style implied content" copy.

A postcard from Intech, a gear manufacturer, has this headline on the advertising side of the card:

"How to Stop Teeth in Your Plastic Gears from Breaking."

Engineers read and responded to this postcard, because the headline offers a benefit they are seeking.

"How to" is a strong phrase in "editorial-style implied content," because it promises useful tips, ideas, or instructions.

The body then delivers the promised knowledge in a series of short bullets. Including:

- "Understand the loads on the gear—-our free Gear Card summarizes the load data."

Engineers know what loads are and that they are important.

Copy tells them how to get the data they need:

"For your FREE Gear Card call or visit URL."

- "Select the right plastic."

The engineer learns that the characteristics of the ideal plastics for gears include dimensional stability in moisture and secure attachment to the shaft.

On the reverse side of the postcard is the headline:

"Only Power-Core plastic-on-metal gears give you all these advantages."

Then a short bullet list of copy reveals that Intech's gears possess all of the characteristics needed to prevent the teeth from breaking off.

Including;

- No moisture absorption = no swelling.
- Metal core dissipates stress and heat to reduce thermal expansion.
- Intech helps you size the gear correctly for the load.

At the bottom is the offer:

"Intech engineers can help you size the gear to last in your application based on the load. For your FREE Gear Card call or visit URL."

This specific copy technique used in the Intech postcard is called "setting the specs," and it has two parts.

First, it educates the reader on the specifications and features to look for when buying gears whose teeth won't break off.

Then, it shows that only Intech, with its unique gear design and engineering capabilities, makes a gear that meets all the specs.

If the reader checks other gears against these specs, no other gear meets them, making Intech's value proposition unique.

So the engineer who finds the specs sensible and believable buys the Intech gear, because only Intech meets them.

# CHAPTER 45

# Boost Conversion With an Autoresponder Email Series

"Gating content [putting it behind a landing page or form] isn't the problem," writes marketer Brian Cohen in a recent LinkedIn post, "it's what you do with the contact information after."

Some B2B marketers don't do nearly enough to make the names and email addresses of those who click on their ads and landing pages more productive and profitable.

In particular, they ignore this extremely effective conversion-boosting technique:

*Namely, to automatically send via autoresponder a series of follow-up emails to everyone who submits their name and email address.*

Purpose: to convert the maximum number of inquiries to qualified sales leads.

This neglect in lead nurturing is especially prevalent with prospects who have given you their information in order to download, say, a free white paper or some other informative and valuable content lead magnet.

So, how do you structure a follow-up autoresponder email sequence to improve conversion from clicks to qualified leads?

Typically, we use a classic email responder sequence for follow up that has 7 efforts and has a messaging sequence something like this one:

- *Email #1*: Thank them for their inquiry. Remind them of why they requested your material, including the problem it solves, the solution it presents, and what makes that solution different and better than others.
- *Email #2:* Repeat essentially the same key points you stated in email #1, using new wording that amplifies and clarifies those points, and adding one or two new sales points.

Why the repetition? Because people click quickly and often without much thought, and then may not remember contacting you in the first place.

So it's important to remind them that *they* contacted *you*—so they do not think they are being spammed.

- *Email #3:* Encourage them to read your lead magnet; stress the value and benefit of doing so; and also point to one specific and valuable tip it contains; and reference the page number on which that tip appears.

- *Email #4:* Again, encourage them to read your lead magnet by pointing to a second useful and interesting tip, fact, or idea; and don't forget to reference the number of the page on which it appears.

- *Email #5:* Say what your product or service can do for them, and add a call to action, such as a discovery call, estimate, needs assessment, quote, or free consultation.

- *Email #6:* Get them to respond now instead of later by using an urgency device such as a deadline, limited supply, discount pricing, free bonus, or time-limited special offer.

- *Email #7:* Offer additional content that goes beyond or amplifies what is covered in the lead magnet; e.g., invite them to a free webinar, product demonstration, or to your exhibit at an upcoming industry trade show.

The objectives your autoresponder email sequence should accomplish include:

- Make sure they understand that you are fulfilling their inquiry.

- Engage them with the content they requested from you.

- Educate them about your value proposition as it relates to their needs.

- Promote a next step or call-to-action.

Your goals:

- Maximize conversion.

- Have a sales conversation.

- Get an order so they become a customer.

# CHAPTER 46

# Integrating Online and Offline With "Chicken Feed"

A headline, published in the 10/18/22 issue of *CMO Briefing* by xiQ, boldly forecast:

> ***"56% of B2B Marketers to Go Mostly Or Entirely Digital Within a Decade."***

Well, for those of us who are true multichannel marketers, and adroitly integrate both online and offline tactics into our campaigns, that's good news.

Copywriter Paul Bringe once said of direct mail: "When the feed is scarce, the chickens will scratch at anything."

And if you think of direct mail as "feed," then the feed in your prospect's mailbox has gotten scarcer as of late.

Forbes reports that "as small businesses experiment with alternative forms of advertising, the volume of direct mail is slowly declining."

According to the United States Postal Service, annual advertising mail volume fell from 103.5 billion DM pieces mailed in 2007—to just 66.2 billion pieces in 2021—a drop of 36%.

This means that there are fewer direct mail pieces in the mailbox fighting for the prospect's attention.

And with less feed, the chickens are scratching more than ever—and as a result, response rates have been steadily rising in recent years, as Adweek and others report.

Which is an opportunity for those of us who embrace DM to gain a leg up on the half or so of B2B marketers that are cutting down or dropping print DM altogether—and, I would argue, at their peril.

"Seems strange," comments CMO David P. "As there is less competition in the mailbox these days, now would be a great time to crash the box and get some attention with a series of quality packages with a strong offer."

David adds: "Everybody's pixel crazy, it's all about funnels . . . I'll match results with a solid control DM package to a great list every time!"

Marketing consultant Greg K. advises: "When everyone else is crowding the inbox, make some noise in the mailbox."

Marcom manager Charles C. posits that "these days direct mail is a 'disruptive technology', and done well could get more attention than digital communications."

This may give an advantage to marketers with gray hair, because we—unlike our millennial counterparts—know and are comfortable with direct mail.

Copywriter Neil G. says, "I find a general reluctance among a younger crowd of marketers to take advantage of the uncrowded mail field."

And to a degree, I find their caution warranted.

Yes, direct mail packages can perform well in both solo promotions as well as integrated into multi-channel campaigns.

But, when your DM package bombs, that hit to your pocketbook can sting more than an email or Facebook ad that doesn't work.

My advice:

Educate yourself on what works in direct mail.

Or, get help from others who already know.

Now. that still doesn't guarantee your DM piece will be a winner.

But it can help tip the odds of success in your favor.

# CHAPTER 47

# The 10/10 Rule of "Aspirational Advertising"

"Aspirational marketing" refers to advertising that targets your prospects not by who they are, but by who and what they want to become.

For instance, I would wager that most of the prospects for Peloton don't look anything like the fitness models using Peloton exercise equipment in its TV commercials.

The actors in the Peloton spots have great bodies. They go "balls to the wall," exerting themselves to the maximum when they work out—and, they seem to enjoy it.

That's deliberate, of course, because the hard bodies in the Peloton TV advertising are what Peloton believes its ideal potential customers aspire to be.

The 10/10 rule of aspirational marketing has been used for decades in exercise, fitness, weight loss, fashion, and beauty advertising.

Simply put, the people you show in your advertising should be about 10 years younger and 10 pounds lighter than your actual customers and potential customers.

Prospects universally aspire to be thinner and more youthful in appearance. But why specifically 10 years and 10 pounds?

Because 10 years and 10 pounds is enough of a difference to be desirable and aspirational. Yet at the same time realistic enough to be seen as attainable.

According to an article in *The Drum* (9/13/23), only 4% of people in ads are over the age of 60, despite the fact that Americans age 60 and older control 25% of consumer spending.

*The Drum* editors see this as being a bad thing: They say it is ageism—and a failure to be inclusive.

What *The Drum* writers may be missing is that many aging boomers wish we were more attractive and trimmer. And we also prefer looking at images of more attractive and youthful actors and models. Rather than plain folk who look, well....like us.

Now, there is an opposing and upcoming school of marketing that takes the opposite approach of aspirational marketing: "reality-based marketing (RBM)."

The theory behind RBM is that you engage your prospects more powerfully by showing them reality.

This reality includes images of people who look and seem to be like the prospect—and NOT the idealized versions depicted in aspirational advertising

For decades, the Victoria's Secret catalog was the gold standard of aspirational advertising—so packed with glamour photos of hot models that some jokingly referred to it as "the Christian man's Playboy."

Today, Victoria's Secret has deep-sixed the steamy sex appeal super-models in favor of a broader and more inclusive selection of models, ranging from fit and slim to stocky and even overweight.

In a recent email (9/14/23), copywriter Brian Clark writes that "crafting messages from your personal point of view can backfire spectacularly if you're not aligned with your intended audience's worldview, values, and attitudes."

As a marketer, you have to understand your market well enough to know which approach would works best: reality-based marketing or aspirational advertising. And that includes knowing who your market really is.

For instance, Victoria's Secret catalogs always appealed to men, because men like woman with hot bodies wearing skimpy lingerie.

But are the Victoria's Secret customers women who wear the lingerie—or men who want their women to wear it?

If the company's customers are mostly the women who wear the product, then the question is: what images will generate more engagement and online orders?

The sexy bikini models of aspirational advertising?

Or a broader and more inclusive spectrum of reality-based women of all shapes, sizes, and colors?

# CHAPTER 48

# Selling from Strength

According to an article in *eCommerce*, 95% of all businesses fear recession.[3]

The problem is that when you are selling from a position of fear, you are selling from a position of weakness.

Your prospects can "smell" the "stink" of that fear on you, which weakens you, making you less effective as a seller and marketer.

The good news is that there are 4 proven tactics for combating both perceived and real weakness. They can empower you to once again sell effectively from a position of strength, with confidence, and by doing so, improve your sales and marketing ROI:

## #1: The Silver Rule of Marketing.

The Silver Rule of Marketing is that it is better for your prospects to come to you, rather than for you to go to them.

Why is it better?

When prospects come to you, they are ostensibly more qualified.

Just by virtue of having sought you out, the prospects have already, to some degree, shown they have a real problem they want to solve.

And also by coming to you, they have additionally indicated some level of preference or inclination to get that solution from you.

Content marketing is one of today's biggest go-to Silver Rule strategies. You know how it works:

The prospects read your content … become convinced that you know what you are talking about … and then inquire about how you can  help them implement the ideas in your article or paper.

---

3   https://www.linkedin.com/pulse/95-businesses-fear-recession-marketing-budget-cuts-likely-blazewicz/?trk=pulse-article

### #2: The Busy Dr. Syndrome.

For a medical appointment, it can be frustrating to walk into an overly crowded waiting room—but it can be even more off-putting to walk into an empty waiting room.

Why? Because absence of patients makes you question whether the doctor can be any good at what she does.

The Busy Dr. Syndrome simply says that customers would rather do business with vendors who seems busy and successful—rather than those who seem needy and desperate.

So even if you are worried by recession to the point where you sometimes feel a desperation to close a sale—don't let it show. Ever.

Always say you are busy and successful. Follow the old age: "Never let them see you sweat."

### #3: The Double Pipeline.

Another way to never be or feel needy is to NOT actually need to make the sale.

That's where the "Double Pipeline" can give you this advantage. Here's how and why it works:

Most business owners make the mistake of doing just enough marketing to keep their lead pipeline full—producing enough leads to keep the business afloat—but no more than that.

However, when some of your leads don't close, you then don't have the level of work, orders, and income you really wanted or need.

The Double Pipeline says you should do TWICE as much marketing as you think you need to keep your lead pipeline full.

That way, even if half of the opportunities go south, you STILL have the volume of orders and deals you need to stay solvent and profitable.

### #4: The Takeaway Close.

When a prospect keeps pushing back as you are trying to close the deal, do a sudden turnaround and say:

"You know what? Perhaps this isn't really for you." And close your laptop and get up from the table to end the call.

You will have just instantly shifted from making your product easy to get to making it hard to get.

This is called the "takeaway close."

It works for this odd reason: once you tell people they can't have something, they instantly want it more.

Strange but true!

# CHAPTER 49

# DM Response Boosters That Worked Like Gangbusters

A traditional B2B direct mail package consists of an outer envelope, sales letter, brochure, and reply element.

But you can often boost response by adding yet another element to the mailer. Here are 7 that have worked well for me and my copywriting clients over the years:

### #1: "Mist Eliminator Enclosed."

We were selling a pollution control device—a mist eliminator—made of knitted metal.

The mailer consisted of a small sample of the knitted metal material.

The sales letter was printed to look like a shipping tag and tied to the metal sample.

The outer envelope read "FREE Mist Eliminator Enclosed."

Findings: samples of products, sections of products, or materials are effective.

Reason: they add bulk to the envelope, and they grab the recipient's attention.

### #2: RFP enclosed.

A mailer selling industrial mixers included a simple form the recipient could use to request a proposal and quote on equipment for his application.

It generated more qualified inquiries and better closing rates, because the prospect provided the manufacturer with the key information they needed to quote on the best mixer for the job.

### #3: "Burn This Coupon."

A chemical company selling a fireproofing compound coated a sell sheet and reply coupon with the product.

The copy then invited the prospect to try burning the flier—which didn't burn, demonstrating that the product works.

### #4: "Brick" mailer.

A construction company sales manager sent prospects a brick in the mail with his business card silkscreened on it.

When he followed up with a phone call, and the assistant asked who was calling, he said, "Tell him I'm the guy who sent him the brick."

### #5: "Sticker shock" PDR.

Physicians' Desk Reference sent a mailer offering the new edition to previous buyers who owned older editions—based on the proposition that the customer's current PDR wase now out of date.

In the mailer, the publisher enclosed an adhesive label and told the recipient to stick on their current book. The message on the label: "Warning: This PDR is Out of Date and Should Not be Used for Prescribing."

It worked because the label dramatized the proposition in a tangible way with interactivity when the recipient peeled off the label from the mailer and affixed it to the book. Result: triple the sales of the previous mailers.

### #6: Ad reprint enclosed.

Instead of a sales brochure, enclose a reprint of one of your ads.

The ad is on the front. On reverse side, use an FAQ to answer questions and overcome objections in a plain-speaking way.

### #7: Article reprint enclosed.

Instead of a sales brochure, include a reprint of an informative article you have had published in a magazine or journal.

This works because an article from a publication has more credibility and useful content than one of your sales brochures.

I prefer using a shorter article that can fit one or two sides of a sheet of letter-size paper.

That way, it is informative reading, but not overwhelming reading.

# CHAPTER 50

# Acronyms and Abbreviations

On a recent radio commercial the advertiser said "we are rated A+ by the BBB."

I might have opted to say "rated A+ by the Better Business Bureau."

Yes, BBB and Better Business Bureau are the same thing.

And so it should be equally clear either way.

But when you say "rated A+ by the BBB" it's too many letters strung together, and the listener's mind shuts it out.

"Rated A+ by the Better Business Bureau" is more palatable to the recipient of your message.

Overuse of arcane jargon, little-known acronyms, and unfamiliar abbreviations can stop your readers in their tracks—and not in a desirable way.

It is okay and sometimes even preferred to use acronyms and abbreviations that people are familiar with and whose meanings are clear to them.

But the problem is you can't be sure whether and how many of your readers know them. Let's look at a few example:

- GWP stands for global warming potential. Many people don't know that. And many don't know what it means. Solution: spell out GWP and give a quick definition the first time it appears in your copy. After that, you can use the abbreviation.

- USA is safe. Almost everyone knows it stands for United States of America.

- DARPA is also frequently used. But many don't know what it stands for. They know it is some kind of government agency, but may not understand what DARPA is or does.

- DoD is on the border as far as usage is concerned. Many people know it stands for Department of Defense, and they know what that is. But many others don't. And with the lower case o between the two capital Ds, DoD looks a bit odd, at least to me.

- Laser is a familiar acronym and most people know what a laser is. They don't necessarily know that it stands for. But when a thing is most commonly called by its acronym, it doesn't matter so much. Although when I went for laser eye surgery, and the doctor did not know what laser stands for, I though perhaps he should. But you and I do not need to.

- Technical terms most commonly called by their abbreviation are frequently not written out, especially when the full name is difficult to remember; e.g., LSD and DNA.

- Even if the technical term is a word or phrase and not an abbreviation or acronym, you may want to give a brief definition the first time you use it in your copy. Sometimes we may think everyone in our audience understands the term. But when you ask them to tell you what it means, they cannot give you an articulate answer.

Why such a fuss about abbreviations and acronyms? In Kurt Vonnegut's novel *Cat's Cradle*, the author has a scientist say that if you can't explain a thing to a 12-year-old, you don't really understand it yourself.

So if your reader encounters an abbreviation or word he does not know, that lack of knowledge can severely diminish his comprehension of the text that follows.

The best and safest rule in writing is therefore: *when in doubt, spell it out.*

# CHAPTER 51

# B2B Marketing Channels

When I started out in industrial marketing in the late 70s, both the sales funnel and the marcom tools needed for it were few and far between—and relatively simple.

We created a trade journal print ad offering a free color brochure. We mailed the brochure to the prospects who requested it. Then a sales rep followed up to make the sale.

In addition to brochures and print ads, the other major B2B marcom tools were primarily trade show exhibits, direct mail, postcard decks, press releases, and planted feature articles in the trade journals.

Today, that funnel has largely been supplanted by new multichannel marcom models and methods. But which are the most popular and prevalent?

Veteran copywriter Steve Slaunwhite says, "Recently, I've been doing informal surveys of B2B buyers who are under 30. I ask them to describe their typical buying journey. Here's what they're telling me.

"For a product: Search Google, visit the product description page, read online reviews, talk to a sales rep.

"For a professional service: Search LinkedIn, read a few recent posts of the prospective service provider, visit their website, set up a call or meeting.

"When I ask about email for getting to know the company or professional, staying in touch, getting special offers, product/service updates, etc., they say they prefer social media."

Steve says he found that younger B2B buyers have a growing dislike for email. I have also noticed a growing minority of B2B marketers using SMS texting—both as a follow-up, and less often, as a marketing outreach tactic to cold lead.

Social media, defying my predictions to the contrary, has become a go-to marcom channel—with LinkedIn leading the list. HubSpot[4] says the top channels used by B2B marketers are social media, websites, blogs, and yes, they also still say email.

According to an article in *ANA Business Marketing SmartBrief* (5/31/23), 70% of companies surveyed plan to increase their marketing budgets this year. Of those, 56% are spending that increased budget on social media—their top choice—vs. only 40% on paid search, the #2 choice.

Another phenomenon of note is today prospect's reduced reliance on salespeople. In the 20th century, after the prospect requested a product brochure, marketing  handed off the lead to the sales team, who then provided whatever additional information the prospect wanted to know.

Today, with content-rich B2B websites, the prospect can get a lot further along with his product research on his own, before speaking to a sales rep. In fact, some B2B e-commerce enables customers to place orders online, with no salesperson involvement.

Bottom line: the multitude of marcom tactics, tools, and channels now available to us today makes effective planning of omnichannel B2B marketing campaigns more complex and challenging than ever.

But at the same time, when properly planned and executed, these more sophisticated sales funnels, integrating both print and digital, can often reduce marketing costs, increase sales, and improve ROI.

---

[4]  https://blog.hubspot.com/marketing/marketing-channels

# CHAPTER 52

# Running Your Freelance Copywriting Business

Different copywriters typically operate their writing businesses in one of 7 different ways:

**#1: *Fee-based, project-oriented contract copywriters*.** I am a contract copywriter. Clients hire me to write copy for them on a project basis for a flat fee per project.

This is the simplest, oldest, most straightforward, and most prevalent arrangement.

I have been primarily a fee-based contract copywriter for decades.

For instance, last week, a client hired me to write a simple postcard for $950.

I wrote the copy. Submitted it to my client. And they sent me a check for $950.

**#2: *Fee-based, hourly contract copywriters*.** Similar to #2 above, except the copywriter charges by the hour instead of by the project.

The hourly arrangement can work when the scope of the copywriting work is not yet well-defined or difficult to pin down.

Otherwise, I prefer project pricing, as it avoids surprises when the client gets your bill.

**#3: *Retainer-based freelancers*.** Some freelance copywriters primarily work with clients on a monthly retainer basis.

I have a few clients on retainer, particularly when what they want is both advice and copy, and their needs are frequent and ongoing.

But for most of my clients who use me regularly, we are both happy with fee-based pricing.

**#4: Royalty-based.** Some copywrites have this deal: If their copy works well, they get paid a bonus incentive e.g., a percentage of net revenues generated by the promotion.

This can sometimes work in your favor with more sophisticated direct marketers who measure and track results and revenues your copy generates—and can share their sales reports with you.

But with local and other smaller clients that don't measure and track, if they don't know how many orders your ad produced, then how can they pay an accurate royalty?

**#5: Freelance sites.** Some copywriters, especially but not exclusively newbies, get a lot of their work from freelance sites such as Upwork. Clients post projects they need written on Upwork, and freelancers bid against one another hoping to win the assignment.

I am not a fan of freelance job sites, because the clients posting jobs are often buying based on price and looking for the low bid.

For most service businesses, including copywriting, price buyers are the least desirable clients to have. They are not profitable. And clients who pay the least are often the most demanding and difficult.

**#6: Clientless copywriters.** These copywriters make their money by using their copywriting skills to promote their own products.

They have no fee-based clients, and make their money when their copy generates orders for the products they produce and sell—typically online courses, memberships, training, and other information products.

**#7: Freelance/staff hybrid:** In addition to their freelancing, some copywriters also work full or part-time on staff for a small business, ad agency, or other employer.

*The pro:* a steady stream of income from your "day job" to see you through the peaks and valleys of freelancing.

*The con:* the more of your time your employer is buying, the less flexibility and time you have for freelance clients—which may cause you to lose projects and customers.

# CHAPTER 53

# Increasing Clicks and Conversions

As a direct response copywriter, my primary job is to write copy for my clients that beats their control.

By that I mean it generates more inquiries and orders than their current promotion for the product.

Having been tasked for over four decades with the task of boosting response rates and sales, I've concluded that the following key factors are the ones that matter most:

## #1: Credibility.

Who is the mailer from? A Fortune 500 company? A local know and reputable firm? An MD or RN? A seller whom you don't know personally or have never even heard of?

And don't forget to market to your current customers. Most marketers don't do that nearly enough, given that existing customers are 5X more likely to order from you than strangers are.

## #2: Track record.

How many customers does the seller have? How long have they been in business? How many systems have been installed—and how well have those performed in the field?

Does the seller have good online reviews? Have they been featured favorably in mainstream media? Any notable achievements or awards?

## #3: Benefits.

Does the product or service provide clear and specific benefits? Are these benefits ones that customers desire? Are they major benefits or minor ones? Are these benefits different and better than those your competitors deliver?

## #4: Systems.

What is the mechanism, system, or operating principles that enable your product to deliver superior benefits and performance?

Even if the methodology is complex, by describing it in a way that sounds right and seems to make sense, you can convince the readers that your product does what you say it will do.

## #5: ROI.

Your copy should present logical arguments, facts, and other credible proof to show buyers they will get a positive return on investment—and the bigger and faster the ROI, the better.

Say I have 5 employees each earning $80,000 a year performing a task manually, making my labor cost $400,000 a year for that function.

If your AI software can automatically do the job without human operators and costs only $40,000 to license, I can stop paying the employees their combined $400,000 annual salary.

Which means within one year, my ROI will be 10:1.

## #6: Offer.

The offer is what customers get when they buy combined with what they have to do to get it.

The ad or mailer's reply mechanism is part of "what they have to do to get it."

For instance, with a postcard mailing driving clicks to your web page, do customers have to type a long URL into their browsers?

Or might it increase response to give them an easy-to-scan Quick Response Code as a second online response offer?

Other important variables in the offer include:

- Products—brands, choices, configurations, options, models, colors, sizes, power, and accessories.
- Price—amazingly, the low price often does not produce as many orders as a higher price—as incredible as it sounds.
- Discounts and bonus gifts.
- Terms—one payment up-front … installment payments … bill-me offers.

The items spelled out here are by no means all-inclusive; for example, I have made no mention of the mailing list, a critical factor that can influence responses enormously.

But the parameters listed above are all, to some degree, things you, as a marketer, can usually control to one degree or another.

CHAPTER 54:

# Getting Started as a Copywriter

To launch yourself as a copywriter, there are two essential steps: First, learn how to write copy. And second, once you can write copy reasonably well, find copywriting assignments as a freelancer.

You do not need a college degree. And, if you do have or pursue a B.S. or B.A., you do not have to major in English, journalism, advertising, marketing, or other related fields.

In fact, I recommend that you instead major in political science, economics, computer engineering, geology, biology, and other expert subjects—all of which can give you the background to write for industries related to your major.

For instance, a degree in petrochemical engineering is ideal for writing copy about the oil and gas industry.

College aside, there are four activities that are the foundation of your real copywriting education: writing, reading, courses, and paying attention to ads—and none of these require a formal education.

### Writing

The best way to learn how to write is by writing a lot.

For instance, Malcom Gladwell says that if you write or do anything else for 1,000 hours, you become good at it.

When I was in college, I majored in chemical engineering. But I also wrote for the campus newspaper, which was a daily.

By the end of my senior year, I had written for more than a thousand hours. I wasn't great, But I was competent.

The combination of writing experience and engineering education landed me several corporate job offers as a technical writer.

## Reading

Most writers are inveterate readers. There are two types of reading materials we consume.

First, we read a ton of source material for specific writing projects. When writing about dietary supplements, for instance, I read clinical papers on each ingredient used in the formulation.

Second, we read widely on just about everything else. In this way, your mind becomes a vast storehouse of knowledge on topics of all kinds, and the information continually finds its way into whatever you are currently writing.

## Courses

The best training for copywriters is not college courses. It is books, ebooks, online master classes, trade publications, blogs, videos, webinars, podcasts, and other educational materials you can find online. All you need do is Google "copywriting" and you will find more material on the topic than you could consume in a lifetime.

Again, these are not college courses. They are training programs taught by practicing copywriters.

The problem with college marketing professors is that some (not all) are merely theoreticians. But copywriting is a practical skill, and at the end of the day, results are all that matter.

## Ads

Perhaps the best education you can get in copywriting is by studying what's working today in the particular niche or field in which you write.

You do this by paying attention to, reading, and analyzing the marketing messages delivered to you each day by email, online ads, direct mail, TV, Facebook, Google, and other marketing channels.

When you get a promotion you feel is particularly strong, engaging, or interesting, keep a copy in a "swipe file." Meaning a file of advertising you may want to consult for ideas and inspiration when writing copy for your clients.

Tip: If you get a particular promotion multiple times, mark it in your swipe file as such. The repetition is noteworthy, because it means the copy is working. If it was not working, the marketer would not keep repeating it.

# CHAPTER 55

# Five Ways to Get New Copywriting Clients

Once you learn to write copy reasonably well, the next step in launching your freelance copywriting practice is to find clients who want to hire you to do writing projects.

There are five primary sources for getting new clients: (a) starter jobs, (b) personal branding, (c) lead generation, (d) networking, and (e) cold calling.

## Starter jobs

Your first freelance jobs are likely to come from "low-hanging fruit"—meaning they are within your grasp to win, even if you are a beginner with little or no experience.

For instance, say your Uncle Bob owns a pizza restaurant. Offer to write an appealing take-out and delivery menu.

Or a contractor you use for home repair complains that business is slow. Offer to write a mailer that can help attract new customers.

These are relatively easy clients to get. They know you. They are local. Small. Not terribly sophisticated about marketing. And their projects are usually simple to write.

Don't worry so much about how much you will get paid. You are doing these starter jobs primarily for the experience. To get samples for your portfolio. And also to get client testimonials.

## Personal branding

"Personal branding" encompasses activities that help build awareness and position you as an expert in your field, industry, or niche; e.g. automobiles, finance, software, social media, or whatever.

For instant, I gave a talk on marketing at a meeting of the Newsletter Publishers Association, a trade group for newsletter publishers.

Right after my talk, an audience member approached me and hired me on the spot to write two direct mail package to sell subscriptions to a couple of his publications.

Among the activities available in your personal branding arsenal are:

- Blogging.
- Writing articles.
- Articles written about you in the media.
- Press releases.
- Being a podcast guest.
- Appearing on radio and TV shows.
- Pubic speaking.
- Webinars.
- Teaching at a local college.
- Social media.

And that's just the tip of the iceberg. Any others can you think of to add to my list?

## Lead generation

"Lead generation," also called "demand generation," refers to any marketing communication created with the goal of generating sales leads—defines as inquiries from qualified prospects.

Some examples include:

- Print—newspaper and magazine ads, direct mail, door hangers, billboards, transit advertising, and package inserts.
- Digital—Google and Facebook ads, banners, email blasts, e-newsletters, landers, and YouTube videos.

## Networking

"Networking," colloquially referred to as "schmoozing," is at its most basic, going to venues where your potential clients gather, and engaging in conversations with them.

Your ultimate goal is to meet people who can hire you, speak with them, start building a relationship, and assess whether the person might be a potential customer for your product or service.

Though you can schmooze with people anywhere, one of the most popular venues for networking are meetings of professional societies and associations whose member are in your industry or target market.

### Cold calling

"Cold calling" means getting a list of potential clients with whom you have no relationship, and then phoning them to see whether you can get them interested in hiring you.

A number of freelance copywriters like use cold calling as a method of generating interest and new business. I personally do not, for three reasons:

1. People don't enjoy getting cold called.
2. Making cold calls is often unpleasant and stressful.
3. You are going to be rejected often.

Also, when you are sitting there cold calling, many prospects see you as not being busy or successful—because in their minds, if you were, you wouldn't be dialing for dollars, right?

# CHAPTER 56

# Archetypal Headlines

In an ad, GETTING ATTENTION is the job of the headline.

Through long decades of trial-and-error and testing, we have discovered 7 categories of headlines that work especially well for getting attention.

They are so timeless that we call them "archetypal" headlines:

### #1: Reason-why headlines.

These headlines promise to reveal multiple reasons why the prospects should want to buy the product.

The headline begins with the words "reasons why" and the body copy under it is a numbered list of sales points.

*Examples:*

"7 Reasons Why TV Producers Prefer Unilux Strobe Lighting Systems."

"5 Reasons Why You Can't Afford to Miss the Toronto Money Show."

### #2: Question headlines.

Questions work in copy because, when you ask someone a question, you are actively engaging with them.

Right?

(See how it just worked with you!)

However, question headlines work only if the question is one that arouses curiosity, and to which the reader would want to know the answer.

*Examples:*

"Can Your Write a Letter Like This One?" from an ad selling an AWAI copywriting course.

"When an Employee Gets Sick, How Long Does It Take Your Company to Recover?" for business insurance.

"Is Your Pump Costing You More to Operate Than It Should?" for Gorman-Rupp pumps.

"What Do Japanese Managers Have That American Managers Sometimes Lack?" for a business magazine subscription.

## #3: How-to headlines.

How-to works because people want to learn interesting and useful things—and "how to" signals to them that they will learn such things by reading your ad.

*Examples:*

"How to Win Friends and Influence People"—from an ad selling the Dale Carnegie book; the headline is also the title of the book.

"How to Bake Beans"—from an ad for baked beans.

## #4: Secrets headlines.

As with how-to, "secrets" implies that you will learn something interesting and useful by reading the ad.

But beyond that, "secrets" headlines also possess the added attention-getting power of exclusivity.

Meaning you are going to learn something others do not know.

*Example:*

"The Secret to Moister, Richer Chocolate Cake"—from an ad for Duncan Hines Cake Mix.

## #5: Free headlines.

"Free" is arguably the most powerful word in the English language.

The desire to get something for nothing is nearly universal.

"Free" improves the headline's attention-getting powers while also causing more people to respond.

*Example:*

"Yours Free—Our Gift to You" collectible ad from Alan Shawne Feinstein.

"New Free Special Report Reveals Little-Known Strategy Millionaires

Use to Keep Wealth in Their Hands—and Out of Uncle Sam's" ad from Sterling Foundation Management.

## #6: News headlines.

People have an intense interest in learning about, seeing, experiencing, and getting things that are new.

In his book *The 16-Word Sales Letter,* Evaldo Albuquerque writes that we are "wired for novelty" and that our brains "light up when we see new stuff."

This is simply and easily communicated by using words that tell readers your product or concept is novel; e.g. "New ... new and improved ... just-published ... newly released ... now available ... at last ... breakthrough"—and many more.

*Examples of headlines touting the new and novel:*

"Finally a Caribbean Cruise as Good as Its Brochure" for a cruise line.

"Announcing a painless cut in defense spending" for a defense contractor.

## #7: Command headlines.

Sometimes, a good way to get somebody to do something is to either ask or tell them to do it.

The command headline tells the reader what to do and provide them with a motivation to do it; e.g., "call this 800 number for a free catalog."

*Example:*

"Try Burning This Headline" for Harshaw Chemical.

Harshaw sold a fireproofing compound. The ad demonstrated the product in this way:

The page on which the ad was printed was coated in the fireproofing chemical. When you held a match to the page, it started burning. But when you removed the flame, the page immediately stopped burning.

In this case, the motivation is to satisfy curiosity about the challenge being made—to light the magazine on fire!

# CHAPTER 57

# Sales Enablement

In one of my very first meetings of my career with a new client, the marketing manager casually said, "We don't have a lot of nixies on this mailing list."

I smiled and nodded, but I had no idea what a "nixie" was. Only, by the way she said it, I believe she *expected* me to know it.

Similarly, today you want to know what your team members or clients are talking about. And so, here are some contemporary marketing terms you should be familiar with:

**B2B, B2C, B2G**. B2B is short for business-to-business—marketing that sells products and services to business. B2C is business-to-consumer, which means you are advertising to a consumer. B2G stands for business-to-government; here your prospects are municipal, state, or the federal government.

**ROI**. In marketing, refers to the return on investment refers to the ratio of the revenues generated by advertising. For instance, if you spend $2,000 to run an ad, and it produces total sales revenue of $4,000, your ROI is 2-to-1.

**Marcom**. Short for marketing communications, marcom refers to a wide range of communications used to promote products—everything from PowerPoint presentations and online videos, to webinars and social media, to email marketing Facebook ads.

**Messaging**. A style guide with standard wording of key sales points and themes that can be used in website copy, ads, brochures, and other marketing communications.

**Sales enablement**. Marketing materials that aid salespeople in presenting, explaining, and selling to prospects. Can include PowerPoint presentations, videos, specifications, and manuals.

*Premium*. A free bonus gift the customer gets when he purchase the main product being advertised.

*Collateral*. Materials used to communicate product information to potential buyers and current customers. Examples include on-sheets, advertorials, battlecards, and white papers.

*One-sheet*. Product information on one or two standard size pages. Typical content includes product description, benefits, features, and some specs. Also called a product sheet, data sheet, or sell sheet.

*Brochure*. Similar to a one-sheet in content, but with multiple pages, typically folded into a pamphlet or saddle-stitched—which is stapling sheets of paper together. Typical content includes product description, benefits, features, and some specs for the product.

*White paper*. Where brochures are product sales documents, white papers take a more informational and educational approach; e.g. understanding the chemistry of catalytic reactions.

*Application brief*. A short document, usually a page or two, that details a specific application for one particular product; e.g. using metal tray towers to distill crude in an oil refinery.

*Battlecard*. A "cheat sheet" or sorts given to salespeople to help them effectively present the product to prospects. Typically may include descriptions of the product of various length (e.g., 50, 100, 250 words), common objections and how to overcome them, and frequently asked questions and the answers,

*Advertorial*. An ad written and designed to look and sound like an article and not a sales piece. Advertorials are more informational, while advertising is more blatantly a promotion.

*Attribution*. The ability to determine which promotion generate an inquiry, lead, click, conversion, order or other response. For instance, if you get a phone inquiry, did it come from your ad, radio commercials, YouTube video, or billboard.

*Copy*. Writing that sells a product—e.g., pay-per-click ads, landing pages, TV commercials, direct mail—by generating direct responses or communicating branding messages.

*Content*. Writing and graphics that help sell a product by presenting useful how-to content; e.g., white papers, presentations, special reports, YouTube videos.

CHAPTER 58:

# Salesmanship or Entertainment?

Since time immemorial, or maybe not quite that long, there has been and continues to be a raging debate about the importance of creativity in advertising.

Meaning, should advertising strive to be creative—and specifically entertaining, dramatic, artistic, and funny? So that the ad agencies can win industry awards...and TV viewers can be entertained?

Or should it avoid being creative and cute? And instead be more straightforward, clear, and direct—with the focus on the product and its virtues—with the goal of selling more merchandise?

Here are some guidelines that may be helpful in shaping your approach to the creation of advertising for your particular products, audience, and markets:

- For products sold through such direct response channels—especially those that can be sold directly from an ad or commercial—audiences can skew to age 40 plus.

These older consumers respond well to advertising that help them make an intelligent and informed decision about whether to purchase your wares.

To many of us in the older generations, money-spending is serious business, not something to clown around about.

"Ads are not written to entertain," wrote Claude Hopkins in *Scientific Advertising*. "This is one of the greatest advertising faults. Ad writers forget they are salesmen and try to be performers. Instead of sales, they seek applause."

- For small and medium-size businesses, local as well as many national, awards are a non-starter.

When you are the CEO of your own business, or the manager of someone else's, you are charged with the singular goal of increasing revenues, sales, and profits. So there is no de facto preference for creative advertising. In fact, the more far-out your proposed ad is, the more wary and skeptical the business owners may become of investing in your advertising guidance.

- Madison Avenue agencies that create national ad campaigns for big consumer brands have a reputation for and highly value creativity in advertising.

One reason is that in the ad agency industry, awards are overwhelmingly given to the most creative campaigns—and those awards are desired by ad companies, because winning a Clio causes the agency's star to rise.

- As for younger consumers, a post on *Later Blog*[5] says that Gen-Zers respond best to advertising that entertains them.

Many young people place a premium on being—as old people like me would put it—"hip" and "with it." And so hip and trendy commercials resonate with them.

A study published in the *Journal of Advertising Research* (September 2013) sought to determine whether there is an optimal level of entertainment for advertising.

The study found that most advertisers believe that entertainment in ads is a powerful tool to get consumers' attention and entertaining content can contribute to effectiveness.

However, the study also notes that entertainment does not *necessarily* make an ad effective—and further, too much entertainment could make it less impactful.

Reason: the entertainment distracts the viewer from the brand and its attributes, thereby harming comprehension. The research also confirms that the funniest ads are not necessarily the most effective.

One example of a famous "creative" ad campaign that failed spectacularly was the sock puppets for pets.com.

In about half a year, the company spent more than $60 million on the campaign. And in those 6 months, it generated only $22 million in revenues—making it a big loser on any accountant's ledger.

---

5   https://later.com/blog/gen-z-marketing/

# CHAPTER 59

# Swipe Files

A "swipe file" contains ads, emails, and other copy and content you have collected and saved.

It is called a "file" because you file all of these copy samples in one place where you can easily retrieve them.

To make retrieval easier, I put them in files labeled either by product (e.g., long-distance phone service, gourmet coffee) or media (e.g., emails, websites).

The term "swipe" means you take concepts—headlines, copy, layouts, and offers that caught your eye in the swipe file samples—then then apply them in your own copy.

Notice I said "apply," not "steal." You should not swipe copy word for word. That's plagiarism.

Rather, the swipes serve as idea starters, inspiration, and models to shape your own original copywriting efforts. That's not plagiarism. In the industry, we call it "copycatting." But it is not copying verbatim. And not stealing.

Rather, we are using ideas that inspire us as jumping off points for our own campaigns.

For instance, a promotion for vision dietary supplement had this intriguing headline: "Why bilberry and lutein don't work."

The ad promotes the advertiser's product by knocking two of the most popular nutrients for eye supplements. This headline implies that competitive brands, which are based on bilberry and lutein, must have poor efficacy.

You can apply a swipe to a different product in the same field (e.g. health), though not a directly competitive product.

For a joint supplement, you could for example write: "Why chondroitin and glucosamine don't work." Different product category , different ingredients targeted, but same approach.

Similarly, I had a winner for a CoQ10 pill with: "Why your CoQ10 doesn't work." The client's product used a different form of the molecule that the body absorbs better than the standard form used in many other CoQ10 supplements.

Or, you can apply the idea in a completely different field. Example: for a promotion promoting options trading software, I wrote: "Why your trading software doesn't work … and never will."

An oft-repeated axiom in copywriting is this: "There is nothing new under the sun. But we can describe old things in a new, fresh, and compelling way."

As you collect samples for your wipe file, you may notice that you encounter some promotions multiple times. Mark these particular "multi-samples" with a red X.

Why? The fact that they continue to run means they are working for the advertiser. This is particular true in the offline world, where mailing and media costs are greater than digital.

But it is a good indicator of effectiveness in any marketing channel. So if a promotion is repeated, you can adapt their approach—and put your own spin on it—with greater confidence. The red-X swipes in my file have cumulatively generated over million dollars in revenues.

Traditionally, swipe files are greatly treasured by direct marketers, while branding ad agencies do not employ swipe files widely. Why is this so?

We direct marketers are concerned primarily with making advertising that makes money for the advertiser. We look for our copy to generate more response, leads, and sales than the company's current ads.

When we creatively borrow from promotions that have been well-conceived and executed—especially when a red X in our swipe file tells us they are proven to work—we greatly increase our own chances of producing a successful promotion while avoiding a bomb.

However, some Madison Avenue advertising agencies that create national ad campaigns for big consumer brands often strive not for higher response but rather for creativity.

Well, creativity means originality. And so many general advertisers view swipes as anathema. And it's true that creativity can help get your ad campaign admired and win creative awards.

But adroit use of swipe files and copycatting can achieve something much more valuable: more orders, increased sales, and higher profits.

CHAPTER 60:

# Death of an Elevator Operator

When I was a kid in the 60s, I loved visiting my dad at his insurance office in Paterson NJ.

My mother would go with me, because I was too young to drive.

When we arrived in the building's lobby, we were always warmly greeted by the elevator operator, Joe.

(Back in the day, many elevators in smaller and older buildings were still operated manually, requiring an operator using a big lever to change floors.)

Joe was a nice man and treated me, a young boy, kindly.

But one day, we went to the building.

A shiny, modern new elevator had replaced the manual one.

The new lift was push-button, requiring no operator.

And Joe was suddenly gone, never to return.

This is the downside of rapidly accelerating technological innovation: many jobs become unnecessary—rendering large number of workers obsolete and unemployed.

Some people argue that by performing menial, routine, repetitive, or boring tasks, automation frees workers to do more "rewarding" and even "creative" work.

But from first-hand observation and experience, I know the sad fact is this, many of these workers do not WANT to lose their jobs.

And many never recover financially from that loss.

You see, at least since the Industrial Revolution, there have been people who are worried about technology advancing to the point where a machine can do their job.

And in fact, for many centuries, such machines have been used to do just that.

For instance, when several of his factory workers formed a union, Thomas Edison responded by building thirty machines to automate their work.

The new factory automation made the laborers obsolete; Edison promptly fired them and said, "The union went out. It has been out ever since."

Today many argue that, so far, the economic growth that results from a move forward in technology has benefited society as a whole, even if certain trades are disrupted in the process.

Unlucky for those trades for sure, but better for society as a whole.

Well, their logic is undeniable.

But at the same time, it just seems heartless.

# CHAPTER 61

# Write It Down

This is old, simple, and basic advice—and 97.9% of the people I know ignore it.

Namely: Always have a pen and pad on you to write things down.

What things?

All the things important enough that you want to capture them for later reference.

Things you see. Things you read. Things you hear.

Observations. Ideas that form as a result of deliberate pondering.

Thoughts that pop randomly into your brain. Questions you have. And any answers that come into your mind.

When you think of something, write it down

Why is having a pad and pen for capturing these ideas important?

Well, you encounter, imagine, or think of ideas, information, and things you want to do, make, or experience all the time.

But if you don't write down the important ones, you will soon forget them.

Ane once you forget, then a great opportunity, wonderful experience, or clever solution may be lost to you forever.

And you'll kick yourself for it.

So have a pad and pen handy—always.

Now, I know of you may be thinking: "I have a smart phone, Bob. So what do I need a pen and paper for"?

Well, by all means, use the tool or medium your prefer: pen and paper, smartphone, tablet, digital recorder, crayon, laptop, quill and parchment, chisel and stone, or whatever.

The only tool you can't and should not depend on is the most fragile: the human memory.

Do not leave things to memory—and risk having a brilliant, valuable idea, thought, action plan, notion vanish into the ether.

Always write it down. Always.

Also, when you encounter something online you want to remember, don't just copy it to your hard drive—but also print a hard copy.

Then tape the printout to your wall, pin it to a bulletin board, or file it in your file cabinet—either alphabetically or just one current folder labeled "ideas."

You'll be glad you did.

P.S. In addition, keep a pad and pen on the nightstand next to your bed, so you can write down ideas that come to you while you are resting or sleeping.

CHAPTER 62:

# The Joys of Copywriting

Just about everyone selling copywriting courses talks about the benefits of becoming a freelance copywriter—such as more money ... no boss ... no 9-to-5 job ... work at home ... no commute ... live wherever you want ... set your own schedule ... travel ... and so on.

But for me, they miss the boat, because my favorite thing about being a freelance copywriter is ... writing copy!

You see, I love the work ... and am grateful that I get to do something I love every day of the week.

The "joys of copywriting" for me include....

1:  Getting to write about interesting things.

2:  Doing research, reading, and learning about the interesting things I have to write about.

3:  Writing the first draft and in doing so creating a piece of writing that has never existed before.

4:  Editing and reworking; I enjoy revisiting the copy and making it the best it can be.

5:  The satisfaction of reading the finished draft—and being confident and content that I know I did a good job.

5:  Seeing a good designer transform my copy into a finished ad, mailer, email, or landing page.

6:  Getting intelligent feedback from the client and other reviews that strengthen the copy when I incorporate those changes.

7:  Holding the finished promotion in my hands, and seeing it get distributed in its final form.

8:  Watching the responses come in and the sales curve moving up.

9:  Getting testimonials and repeat orders from satisfied clients.

10: Knowing my copy has convinced many people to try and therefore benefit from products I believe or know to be good quality and good for them.

Many copywriters confide in me that they hate writing copy—and would loaf, play golf, or drink.

Okay. Maybe I'm the odd duck.

But for me, the writing of the copy is the primary reward …a pleasure to be savored, and not—as some see writing—and unwholesome mental chore to be avoided at any cost.

I have often quoted Noel Coward in my newsletter as saying: "Work is more fun than fun."

For me, that's true: the work is the fun … writing copy that generates a great response rate for the client is the reward for me and them.

Anything else is mainly gravy.

Do I really love copywriting?

Of course.

As Dennis Quaid says to Topher Grace in the movie In Good Company: "Why else would I do it?"

Copywriting course purveyors brag endlessly about how much money they make and can help you make too.

Yes, money is important.

But if money is your primary goal, there are other—and probably better—ways to amass a big pile of it.

Everything from being an investment banker or orthodontist, to starting an e-commerce business or a hedge fund.

One more thing.…

Some senior copywriters reduce the amount of writing they must do by subcontracting much of their copy to junior writers—or even by using ChatGPT.

They then polish up the subcontractors copy, slap their own name on it, and submit it to the client as if it was all written, start to finish, by one person.

I have been writing copy for more than 4 decades, and I have never, not even once, subcontracted any client copywriting assignment to a junior copywriter—or any other ghostwriter.

When a client gets copy from me, they know that, for better or worse, every word was written by me—which is after all why they hired me in the first place.

Nothing inherently  wrong with pawning off the work to an anonymous junior copywriter, I suppose.

But that's not the way I roll.

# CHAPTER 63

# Why I Don't Write Books in 7 Days

I see an increasing number of online ads that make this promise:

"Write Your Book in 7 Days."

My concerns with this notion are as follows:

- First, it's all about speed—and nothing about quality.
- Second, yes, some people can write books quickly—but many others who attempt to do so turn out crap.
- Third, what's more important—getting your book on Amazon in a week … or simply writing a darn good book?

Over the past 4 decades, I've written more than 100 books—the vast majority for traditional publishing houses.

My PRIMARY object was never to use the book to promote myself, nor to build a funnel.

My compulsion is simply this….

Whenever I learn something, I feel compelled to pass the knowledge on to others.

And to do that, I write a book on it.

I freely admit that I don't necessarily write the best book in the world on that topic.

But, I always write the best book I can on that topic.

For me to do otherwise would be to cheat the reader.

I would be taking his money for an inferior product—and also wasting his time.

But that's how a dinosaur like me views it.

Many people who want to write a book feel much differently.

How about you?

# CHAPTER 64

# Foner's Boner

I opened a recent email from the *New York Review of Books*—and this quote from Pulitzer Prize-winning historian Eric Foner leaped off the screen and into my face:

"We can't accept the principle that the way to judge a course of study is by how much money you will make."

But, that seems to be how legions of both course sellers and their students judge programs today, right?

Especially (and naturally) when the topic is copywriting, freelance writing, book publishing, teaching, online marketing, real estate, or other subjects where the skills and knowledge gained are intended to yield a profit for the student.

But, are students right to focus on money first? Or missing the broader purpose of learning?

My FB friend JB says: "Foner's is a great sentiment, particularly for people who can pay cash for whatever course of study they choose. But if you're going to go into debt to study, it better not only pay for itself, but also for you to live! Otherwise the rest of us, and society have to pay your debt without getting the benefit of the education."

JT: "I think Foner hit the nail on the head, because monetary goals aren't the only reason people embark on a course of study."

JN: "Depends on the subject matter. A course on wine, art history, philosophy, or theology is primarily about enjoyment or enlightenment. But a course in one's field needs to pay for itself. Even here the benefits may be indirect and hard to monetize."

GD: "How much money someone makes is definitely one way to judge success off of writing. I've seen my byline in newspapers. It's a thrill. But

I would rather have secure finances into the future than see my name in print anymore."

JM: "Foner is correct in principle. Unfortunately, we have turned our institutions of higher learned into glorified tech schools where ROI is the only thing that matters. Personally, I would say a 'class' is something you might take to increase your earning. A 'course of study' is more for personal enrichment that has nothing to do with dollar signs."

ML "If your goal is to make a certain level of income, money would be an appropriate criteria. Personally, I judge its value by whether a program will bring me closer to my priorities."

And SJ opines: "I think it would be better to say, 'We shouldn't accept the principle that the ONLY way to judge a course of study is by how much money you will make.'"

In college, I had two friends, JB and EY.

JB often said: "I love learning!"

But EY had a different priority. He told me, "Bob, my only interest is to turn one dollar into two dollars, as fast as I can, as often as I can."

So, has Foner made a boner and missed the boat? Or has he hit the nail on the head? What does education mean or do for YOU?

# CHAPTER 65

# How to Make Self-Talk Work for You

How can you make self-talk actually work for you?

Positive thinking guru Jon Gordon, in his weekly newsletter (12/26/22), explains the simple secret of effective self-talk:

"Talk TO yourself instead of LISTENING to yourself. Instead of listening to your complaints, fears, and doubts, talk to yourself with words of truth and encouragement."

**Recommendation:** When a negative thought enters your mind, immediately replace it with its logical opposite, which is the strongest positive truth you can think of.

For instance, let's say that because of age, health, or property tax increases, you are reluctantly considering downsizing—and it's making you sad, because you do not want to move.

**Self-talk solution:** Change your attitude of resentment and unhappiness at having to leave the home you love, to an attitude of gratitude; e.g., "We have been so lucky to have lived here and enjoyed our wonderful home all these years."

But to make that work, you have to practice this method of self-talk consistently—day after day.

Sometimes you will convince yourself. Find comfort. Reduce negative thinking and feelings. It will work. And you will feel better.

Other times, especially if you are new to this kind of self-talk, you may find you don't have the will power to embrace it.

The secret is practice—constant and diligent application of the method.

It's similar to muscle memory you build up working out at the gym.

Practicing self-talk as Gordon describes it makes your "mental muscles" stronger—giving you greater control over your thoughts..

My biggest complaint with so many self-help books I have read tell you the "secret" to success is positive thinking.

But most do not tell you HOW to be a positive thinker.

Therefore, those books are telling you WHAT to do, but not HOW to do it.

Which is inadequate writing for a how-to book—and of extremely limited value.

CHAPTER 66:

# Too Much of a Good Thing

For more than half a century, I've been a rabid superhero fan.

Buying and collecting both Marvel and DC, starting when I was age 12; at the time, these comic books sold for 12 cents per issue.

I read *Superman...Batman...Green Lantern ...Flash...Iron Man... Luke Cage...Dr. Midnight...Spider-Man...Dr. Strange... Avenger... Hulk...the Metal Men...Aquaman... X-Men...*and many others.

In 1979, I saw my first superhero movie on the big screen—*Superman*, starring Christopher Reeve.

I was jazzed, because it heralded the coming of a new generation of great superhero movies that are still being churned out today.

However, as much as I was enamored with superhero movies...

Eventually there were so many, I—to my astonishment—actually grew tired of them—and gradually lost interest.

There's a glut of superhero movies, and as quantity has increased, qualify has suffered.

Today, I skip most superhero movies—and also most superhero TV shows.

I did watch the new Robert Pattison *Batman* on cable—not bad, but for me, a half hour too long.

I was tempted to see *Black Adam*; in particular, I like the casting of Pierce Brosnan as Dr. Fate.

But I did not, as I was repelled by bad reviews and the trailers.

Ditto for the Flash, a superhero I really like.

My favorite superhero show of all time: the original *Adventures of Superman*.

George Reeves will always be the true Superman in my eyes.

# CHAPTER 67

# Do You Hate Getting Telemarketing Calls?

A telemarketer called me with a pitch—I don't remember what it was for.

Whatever it was, I was not interested—and immediately told him so.

He asked, "May I say something?"

I replied: "no."

And then he continued talking.

I said: "You asked me if you could say something. I said 'no.'

"So why are you still talking?"

Now, I understand telemarketers have a job to do.

They are working at a mostly undesirable job—for not much money.

So most times, I am polite.

But….

With the volume of calls increasing geometrically over the past few years, my patience is wearing thin.

BTW, another telemarketer began by telling me: "DON'T HANG UP!"

In a Facebook post, I wrote that I thought "don't hang up" was a bad opening.

Reason: As soon as I hear it—I hang up.

But a FB friend who runs a call center set me straight.

He informed me that he had tested "don't hang up" many times.

And it always improved results.

There's an important lesson here.

Namely, you can't accurately and reliably evaluate marketing by your subjective judgment.

The only way you can know whether something works or not is to test it.

Your opinion may be wrong.

But numbers are much more accurate and reliable.

The British scientist Lord Kelvin said:

"When you can measure something, and express it in numbers, then you know something about it."

# CHAPTER 68

# Marketing, Advertising, Selling, and PR

I am often asked what the difference is between advertising, marketing, selling, PR, and branding.

My favorite answer, which is not original to me, is an old tongue-in-cheek analogy:

- If a young man who wants to date a woman tells her how handsome, smart, and successful he is—that's advertising.

- If the young man tells his dream date she's intelligent, beautiful, and is a great conversationalist, he's saying the right things to the right person, and that's marketing.

- If the young man persists in saying these things until the beautiful woman agrees to go out with him, that's selling.

- If someone else tells the young woman how handsome, smart, and successful her suitor is—that's PR.

- And if everyone already thinks that young man is successful, handsome, and witty—that's branding.

There's another version of this concept that goes something like this:

*If the Circus is coming to town and you paint a sign saying "Circus is coming to Fairgrounds Sunday," that's Advertising...*

*If you put a sign on the back of an elephant and walk him through the town, that's Promotion...*

*If the elephant walks through the Mayor's flower bed, that's Publicity...*

*If you get the Mayor to laugh about it, that's Public Relations...*

*And if you planned the whole thing, that's Marketing*

Attributed to S.H. Simmons, other sources, my LinkedIn connection Boyd, and my FB friend Clifton.

# CHAPTER 69

# The "Drop in the Bucket" Technique

Subscriber PJ writes:

"Bob, if you are offering a saleable product to your prospect. and if they desire your product, they will buy no matter what. It's already inbred in their brain neurons—a proven fact."

The problem, however, is that it's not a proven fact—and often, it's not true.

People desire many things … but they buy only a small fraction of them.

The main fault with PJ's selling hypothesis is that it ignores copywriter Mike Pavlish's "drop in the bucket" trick.

Namely: The prospect may want what you are offering….

But to get him to buy, *you MUST convince him that your price is a "drop in the bucket" compared to the enormous value the buyer will received.*

One of the best ways to do this is to show the great ROI your product will generate for the buyer.

Example: Copy selling success, skill-building, or money-saving books often says:

"We guarantee the book will generate (or save you) 10X its purchase price. If not, return it for a full refund."

Bottom line: you don't make the sale by giving your prospects their money's worth.

You make sales by giving customers more than their money's worth—more than they have any right to expect.

# CHAPTER 70:

# Emotion vs. Logic

An article in *ANA SmartBrief* (11/23/22) states: "In all marketing, your target audience is another human being ... and behind every person, there are emotions."

But when you are marketing technical products—in particular, industrial equipment, subassemblies, and components) ....

...and selling them to technical buyers—e.g., engineers, programmers, IT professionals,, and scientists audiences ....

Then how important in the prospect's decision-making process are emotion vs. logic?

There are two schools of thought concerning this issue....

- *Emotional:* Those who say emotions dominate—even for industrial products—argue that, though the customer may be an engineer, he or she is also a human being first and foremost ... and therefore driven more powerful by emotions than by rational thought—just like everyone else.

- *Logical:* Others say that industrial products must fit the requirements, and performance goals demand for the intended application —therefore, purchase decisions are made primarily based on which product's features and specs are the best fit for the job.

This debate of logic vs. emotion has been going on, especially in B2B marketing, well—since God spoke to Moses.

And when you review industrial product websites, content, and sales collateral, you can clearly see that opinions and practices vary widely.

So, what do you think works best in marketing technical products to technical buyers?

Facts, figures, data, graphs, and other technical information?

Or appealing to the human heart that beats inside every techie?

# CHAPTER 71

# Big Brother Is Watching

The Association of National Advertisers[6] has filed comments with the Federal Trade Commission objecting to proposed new and stricter privacy regulations that aim to stop commercial surveillance.

The FTC defines "commercial surveillance" as "the collection, aggregation, analysis, retention, transfer, or monetization of consumer data and the direct derivatives of that information."

Facebook, for example, is rumored to track and collect 52,000 data points on every one of its 2.7 billion users.[7] [8]

In arguing against these privacy regulations, the ANA stated: "The FTC should not presuppose that any kind of data-informed advertising is harmful without the administrative record necessary to support such a bold assertion."

The total amount of data created, captured, copied, and consumed globally was forecast to increase rapidly and reaching 64.2 zettabytes about 2 years ago, in 2020.[9]

As Rockwell asks in his hit song Somebody's Watching Me, "Why do I always feel like ... somebody's watching me—and I have no privacy?"

Well, Rocky, now you know: big data is a big reason why.

---

[6] ANA Business Marketing Smart Brief, 11/22/22).

[7] https://venturebeat.com/big-data/facebook-should-we-just-be-friends/#:~:text=Facebook%20is%20rumored%20to%20track,data%20points%20on%20every%20user.

[8] https://www.statista.com/statistics/264810/number-of-monthly-active-facebook-users-worldwide/

[9] https://www.statista.com/statistics/871513/worldwide-data-created/

# CHAPTER 72

# The Lifeblood of the American Economy

An article in the *Association of National Advertisers (ANA)SmartBrief* (11/22/22) states unequivocally: "Advertising is the lifeblood of the American economy."

This viewpoint reverberates with ANA members and others of us in marketing, naturally.

But is it really true?

"The lifeblood" means "THE most important thing."

Wouldn't it really be more accurate to say "AN important thing?"

After all, doesn't the answer depend on you, who you are, what you believe, and your point of view?

For instance….

- Copywriters might indeed argue that advertising is the lifeblood of the American economy.
- But software engineers might argue that technology—not advertising—is the lifeblood of the American economy.
- Labor unions might argue that workers—not advertising—are the lifeblood of the American economy.
- Power utilities might argue that energy—not advertising—is the lifeblood of the American economy.
- Ecommerce companies might argue that the internet is the lifeblood of the American economy.
- Engineers might argue that the nation's infrastructure—not advertising—is the lifeblood of the American economy.

- Wall Streeters might argue that money—not advertising—is the lifeblood of the American economy.
- And so on … and so on …

What I am confident in is this: Saying any one particular thing is THE most important is both presumptuous and highly arguable.

Because you are stating it as an absolute … it's an opinion … and you can't definitively prove it.

However, saying a thing is ONE OF the most important things is more credible … more open-minded … and more defensible.

Also, why does the ANA or anyone else feel the need to insist that their thing is number one, with every other thing below that?

Synergistically speaking, isn't the sum of the parts greater than the whole anyway?

# CHAPTER 73

# Somewhere Over the Rainbow Bridge

An ad in AARP Magazine, for a brightly colored Raffinato Murano necklace, has this headline:

"Send Her Over the Rainbow."

The ad is suggesting that you give your wife the necklace, which is resplendent with all the colors of the rainbow, as a gift.

But I have a quibble with the wording "Send her over the rainbow."

My problem with it is that many animal lovers associate the phrase "over the rainbow" with their dead pets going to heaven.

That's largely because of a famous and touching prose poem about it—the Rainbow Bridge.

So when I read "Send Her Over the Rainbow," my mind hears it as hastening someone's death—in this case, the person I'd be giving the ring to.

Not something I consider a selling point.

It struck me in an especially negative way, because Bailey, our beloved Nova Scotia Duck Tolling Retriever, recently passed away.

My colleague SS, disagrees with my interpretation.

"Bob, I would think more than 90% of readers would think the phrase 'over the rainbow' is a beautiful Wizard of Oz reference to a wonderful place where troubles melt like lemon drops. That's a good thing."

But if we are going to quote percentages, you shouldn't ignore that 70% of Americans have a dog or cat.

And I can assure you that many members of this 70% majority of pet owners have heard about Rainbow Bridge.

So in the extreme, my first impression when reading this headline was that it is in essence telling me to "kill your wife."

My Facebook friend YD sees it the way I do: "As a pet lover, I agree. As a woman, the message is foolish. Why would I want to go over the rainbow? No one ever comes back from there."

Another FB friend, OT, notes: "It's a journey of no return."

Meanwhile, another ad in the same issue of AARP Magazine features an unusual piece of costume jewelry: a ring with a faux emerald made from compressed volcanic ash.

The headline reads: "Famous Volcano Has Strange Effect on Women."

Well, I very much like this headline—for these 3 reasons:

- It's specific—unusual, novel, interesting—I haven't heard it before.
- It arouses curiosity. I want to know the name of this "famous" volcano—what its strange effect on woman is … and how it possesses this attribute.
- The headline implies a benefit—that the effect will please the woman I gift it to—which might in turn also work to my advantage.

I did ask my FB friends a specific question about the ad: whether the headline would be stronger if it actually named the famous volcano.

About half, like MM, said naming the specific volcano would make the headline stronger.

Others, like CL, said NOT revealing the volcano's name is stronger, because it would compel them to read further to find out the specific volcano … which, BTW, I suspect is Mt. St. Helen's.

There are strong arguments to be made in favor of either side, and I am sure you can find a few more.

But of course, such a debate can simply be settled by an A/B split test of (a) "famous" vs. (b) the name of the volcano.

# CHAPTER 74

# Is Selling Inherently Scummy?

Subscriber Melvin V. doesn't like my profession.

"I am steadfast against copywriting," he says, because "copywriting is nothing more than creative truths to trick people into purchasing that thing that they surely can't do without."

He sees copywriting and selling as dishonorable professions—and views it practitioners as little better than pond scum.

In my reply, I said to MV: "Your statement shows that you do not understand selling."

But Melvin is not alone in his prejudice.

Many people share MV's believe that selling is inherently unwholesome, distasteful, despicable, deceitful, and unethical.

The truth is, as with almost everything else, some selling is sleazy—and others not.

Here are 5 things you can do to make yours selling more above-board and profitable—even fun:

1: Remember that selling is not trickery. It is at its finest a voluntary value-for-value exchange. A mutually beneficial exchange between two consenting adults—a buyer who wants a product, and a seller who wants to make money helping him get it.

2: The secret to business success is NOT giving the buyer his money's worth—it's giving him more than his money's worth—more than he has any right to expect.

3: In Yiddish, a "mensch" is a person of honor and integrity. When selling, be a mensch, In fact, be a mensch in all you do—including and especially in business.

4: In the movie *Road House*, Patrick Swazey tells his staff (of bar bouncers): "Be nice. Until it's time to not be nice." In selling, be nice always. Problems with a difficult prospect? Don't be not nice. Just walk away.

5: PK, an old sales trainer, told his students the key to success was to have the attitude of "sell 'em ... sell 'em ... SELL 'EM!"

And in a *Twilight Zone* Episode, company president MM tells his underling, "This is a PUSH business ... all the way ... all the time."

I eschew PK's training and MM's management style because they make you seem desperate, needy, and self-centered.

Sales trainer BC takes a different approach: After his presentation, he tells the prospect "you can buy or not buy—and I'm OK either way."

I prefer BC's approach because it signals that you (the seller) are NOT desperate and needy, both of which repel buyers and interfere with making a sale. Also, desperation leaves a scummy residue.

Following these 5 tips will not only make your selling more effective—but you'll also feel more comfortable doing it, too.

On the flip side, an article in *CMO Briefings* proclaims that hard selling is old hat and content—education, conversation, communication are the new sales tools for the 21st century:

"Sales is not about selling anymore, it's about educating and having a conversation. And through that conversation, you place the ideas and receive the ideas."

But wait. At some point, don't you have to close the deal and make the sale?

And even in that conversation, are you only educating objectively, or are you subtly persuading prospects to see your point of view—and if so, isn't that selling?

My colleague KS says: "The 'sell without selling' thing has been around for a while. It's strongly advocated by those who think selling is icky. It's not, and they are wrong."

From another compadre, DG: "Bob, I could not agree more! To be sure, good selling requires in many cases educating the consumer on why the product you are selling is better than the competition. But you MUST ask for the sale. You are leaving money on the table if you don't."

And my close friend DJ adds: "Hog wash. Selling is about selling— it's about structuring a deal expressed as a value exchange. So the perception of both parties is value for value. And that requires the seller to say, 'Here's the cost/price/investment ...and this is what you need to do to get it.'"

What say you?

CHAPTER 75:

# The ROI of College

In *The Week* (9/2/22), Managing Editor Mike Gemein wrote:

"In red states…the very notion of education as anything more than training for efficient work is treated with contempt."

The implication: the primary objective of a college education is to prepare you for a well-paying job.

Lewis Black says as much in the Justin Long film *Accepted*.

Majors commonly viewed as able to achieve that goal include engineering … computer science … pre-med … accounting … and psychology.

And yes, there plenty of liberal arts majors who are also prepared for gainful employment with good compensation.

But the problem today is that the cost of college education is out of control.

For instance, a 4-year undergraduate degree at some Ivy and (what Newsweek has dubbed) New Ivy League schools can run a quarter of million dollars or higher.

As a result, a large number of these graduates need an immediate job and income to start paying back hefty student loans right away.

Now, here are just a few of the reasons why some people are saying to forgo college:

First, it costs a frigging fortune.

Second, it takes a lot of time and effort.

Third, it delays entry into the real world of work.

Fourth, certain fields of study are not promising for finding a good job.

Fifth, some college students party too much—do not take their studies seriously—and in so doing fritter away daddy's money… and mommy's.

President Calvin Coolidge was especially skeptical of the notion that getting a college degree would ensure a person's success.

He famously said of higher education: "The world is full of educated derelicts."

To be fair, there are statistics that support the notion that going to college will deliver a good ROI.

For instance, according to SSA.gov, those with a bachelor's degree earn on average an extra $600,000 to $900,000 in their lifetime than those without college.

But what do you think—should people go to college—or instead get a job….or start a business?

# CHAPTER 76

# The 4-Levels of
# Content Hierarchy

According to *ANA Business Marketing Smart Brief* (10/19/22), 71% of business-to-business marketers say content marketing became even more important in the last 12 months.

But whether those B2B marketers will pay you a decent wage to write content for them is another story.

Freelance writers often ask me, "Does content writing pay?"

My answer is: "Well, no—and yes."

Let me explain.

To begin with, it depends on the level of the content you are writing.

As it  happens, there are 4 levels of content writing:

- **Level 1: Lowest level: "Google Goulash."**
  Mainly articles written for SEO and cobbled together from other articles on the same topics found with quick Google searches.

  Pay: ranges from free—to absurdly low (e.g., $5 for a blog post).

  Some typical Level I topics (from *AARP Webletter* 10/22/22):

  "6 Foods to Skip After 50" …3 Bad Habits for Your Joints" … "10 Common Money Wasters and How to Stop Them" … "8 Things Medicare Doesn't Cover."

- **Level 2: Next level up: freelance articles written for magazines, newspapers, paid subscription newsletters, and content-rich websites.**
  Magazine and newspaper editors hold their freelance writers to a higher standard.

Quality work ... well-written ... well thought out ... thoroughly researched.

Fees vary with the publication; e.g., *The Atlantic Monthly* and *National Geographic* demand better writing, and pay more, than trade journals or your weekly town paper .

Pay for Level II: low to moderate and occasionally more for the top markets—$1 to $2 per word.

- **Level 3: Next up: specialist-written articles on technical topics.**

  White papers and other content on technical and complex topics— written by either by freelance writers or subject matter experts (SMEs).

  These writers and SMEs have experience, expertise, education, or other credentials in the subject or field being written about.

  Example: a colleague of mine has a PhD in chemistry; ghostwrites journal articles for thousands of dollars each—and is constantly in demand.

- **Level 4: High-conversion content—content and copy that directly affects conversion, typically pays more than the other levels.**

  That's because the results can be measured, so if your writing boosts conversions and sales, your client is making money—and therefore is willing to pay more for copy that generate good ROI.

  The highest pay for high-conversion writing is copy for landing pages, or "landers," where the consumer can order the product directly from that page.

  Writing conversion copy for direct online sales pays so well for two reasons.

  First, one of the perils of most other levels of content writing is that you don't always see the direct connection to cashflow.

  But high-conversion landers are profit centers—not a cost centers— that make money for the client.

  So if you write a high-conversion lander that quickly generates

$100,000 in sales, your copywriting fee will be a drop in the bucket compared to the value you deliver.

And second, it pays well because, although there is no shortage of journeyman copy and content writers, relatively few of them can write kick-butt long-copy landers that send sales soaring.

And when your copy actually puts money in your client's pocket, they become far less price-sensitive about your fee.

Because then you can just pose this classic Jay Abraham question to your client: "If I can make you a dollar, will you give me a quarter?"

# CHAPTER 77

# The Case for Plain English

The need to write in plain, simple English is universally recognized by professional writers.

As a copywriter, I am therefore particularly irked when I see writing that seems to be unnecessarily complex.

Especially when I sense, which is often the case, that the writer is doing it deliberately to impress us.

Buckminster Fuller once wrote this awful paragraph:

"Physical points are energy-event aggregations. When the energy-events converge beyond the critical fall-in proximity threshold, they orbit coordinatedly, as a Universe-precessed aggregate."

I call this an example of "What did he say?" writing.

To me, it is pure B.S, piled higher and deeper—ironic, as Fuller didn't even have a PhD, having been booted out of Harvard.

Here's an example of overblown writing from a science book... written for a *lay* audience:

"The fatal legacy of science, as it is unfortunately interpreted in contemporary anthropomorphic culture, is the too frequent insistence that the symbols do themselves constitute a logically autonomous and self-sufficient system, and that in the syntactical structure of that system resides the logical reality that has formerly been supposed to subsist in the extra-linguistic entities symbolized by the system."

Next, take a look at the front-cover headline from the August 2022 issue of *Imprimis* newsletter, published by Hillsdale College:

"The Politicization of the Department of Justice."

Here's why I consider the use of "politicization" a bad word choice:

First, the *Merriam-Webster Dictionary* on my desk does NOT contain the word "politicization."

My dictionary DOES list "politization" and "politicize."

"Politicize" is defined as to make something political, so why not just write "make the DOJ a political issue?"

Second, "politicization" doesn't exactly roll off your tongue.

(And also, to me, it sounds vaguely like it may have something to do with poultry.)

Third, you should write to express, not to impress.

And any way you slice it, you are not impressing anyone with "politicization."

More likely, you are just annoying them.

After reading Hillsdale's "Politicization" headline, my Facebook friend KS commented:

"Even if you don't like the pollution of our language, which I don't either, the language will likely continue to deteriorate—more's the pity."

One more thing…contrary to popular belief, Fuller did NOT invent the geodesic dome.

German engineer Walther Bauersfeld designed a geodesic dome decades before Fuller—and it served as the roof of Zeiss Planetarium in Berlin (source: *New York Review of Books*, 11/22/22, p. 28).

# CHAPTER 78

# On Avoiding "Most"

A quick piece of writing advice:

Be careful about using the word "most" cavalierly.

Why?

Well, when you find yourself writing "most people do X," do you really know that most do X for a fact?

Can you prove it?

A safer alternative is to say "many" instead of "most."

Reason:

"Many" is usually both accurate and believable—the reader finds it credible and therefore is less likely to challenge it.

"Everybody" is similarly problematic.

In a Dilbert cartoon, the Pointy-Haired Boss tells Dilbert: "Everybody hates the code you wrote for this project."

"Really?" Dilbert replies sarcastically. "Everybody? Even Monks in Tibet?"

So, do not write "everybody" does this or that.

Because no, everybody doesn't do it.

Again, just say "many."

Not everybody. Not most.

Both of which are difficult to prove (and often not even true).

Another example of making a statement that's difficult to prove is from a recent TV commercial that says the GMC Sierra is "the most advanced and most luxurious pickup in its class."

Difficult to prove and vulnerable to challenge.

How to fix it:

#1: Cite third-party proof—road tests, data, endorsements; e.g. "Car and Driver magazine calls the GMC Sierra 'the most advanced and luxurious pickup in its class.'"

#2: Rephrase in a way that is easier to defend and therefore less like to be challenged or be met with skepticism; e.g., "The GMC Sierra's performance and luxury are unmatched by any other pickup in its class."

# CHAPTER 79

# Best Call to Action for Radio Ad Response

For decades, the go-to call-to-action (CTA) for radio commercials has been an 800 number, usually repeated 3 times.

Today 800-numbers still remain the preferred CTA for radio.

But an increasing number of radio spots today omit the 800 number—and offer response by web URL or text only.

What do you think of this idea?

My Facebook friends JL says that not having an 800 is bad.

The reason, he says, is that a CTA that requires a URL or text ignores a significant swath of boomers, who are the biggest spenders—CNBC reports baby boomers have 10X more wealth than millennials.

JC comments: "A phone number is hard to remember...but a long website name is impossible to remember."

But AM disagrees: "A URL is fine if it's easy to remember; Chicagoblinds.com is going to be easier to retain than 800-532-1275."

MS: "I think it's a terrible idea. Multiple mechanisms to respond has been shown to win over singular ways."

DM: "Driving in a car listening to radio, it's kind of hard to write down a web or Facebook address, especially if it's a long one. It also profiles what to expect in terms of getting a live voice for help."

"Restricting the CTA to web savvy responders excludes everyone else, says marketing consultant Bob Martel. "If that's the advertiser's intent, they should advertise on the Web."

Bob also says:

1: Most people can recall an 800 number repeated 3 times; not so much a URL.

2: Why text instead of a call? No stand-by operators? Are they screening responses? No dedicated phone line? What text message do they want? What happens after that?

3: The URL is probably a landing page with a longer pitch and another CTA.

BTW, decades ago, when I was a kid, Sheraton ran TV and radio commercials with their 800 number integrated into their jingle…and I still remember it to this day!

Regards,

And please don't email me saying YOU never listen to radio or that nobody listens to radio anymore.

According to MediaTracks.com, 92% of Americans age 18 and older listen to the radio every week.

# CHAPTER 80

# Influencer Marketing

In an episode of the network sitcom *The Neighborhood,* Dave asks Cal:

"Why does your wife only read books recommended by Oprah?"

Cal replies:

"Well, how would she know if the book is any good if it didn't have an Oprah sticker on it?"

This neatly encapsulates the influence that "influencer marketing" has over consumers.

According to the website startupbonsai.com, 80% of consumers have purchased something via an influencer recommendation

Here are 5 things to consider about influencer marketing—and how you might profit from it:

- First, the consumer feels confident about products that get praise— and that praise can include customer testimonials … online reviews … celebrity endorsements … and also influencer recommendations. All can and do work.

- Second, people tend to listen to others whom they know, like, and trust. And they often know, like, and trust the influencers they follow more than they trust you or your brand.

- Third, despite increasing awareness that influencers are quite often compensated by brands in cash, comps, or both for their endorsements—consumers nonetheless still listen to those "paid influencers."

- Fourth, in today's tough economic times, consumers are increasingly risk-averse, wary, cautious, and skeptical. They are less impulsive and weigh purchase decisions more carefully. And so they seek out considerable proof before they buy—and influencer recommendations are often part of that confirmation.

- Fifth, though influencers have been around and mattered for many decades, today they are arguably more prevalent and pervasive than ever. They matter more than ever, because the consumer has become conditioned to question products that are neither endorsed nor supported by a known influencer.

# CHAPTER 81:

# The Secret of "Evergreen Urgency"

An "evergreen urgency" is a call-to-action with an urgency factor that is not tied to a specific date or time limit.

The evergreen offer has a time factor that serves to create a sense of urgency—but that time factor, in fact, applies to every day in the year.

So you can use it anytime you want, all year round.

This classic evergreen urgency offer revolves around the recipient's birthday:

"Enroll before your next birthday"

What makes it an evergreen is that whatever day the recipient gets your email, it is ALWAYS before their "next birthday"—right?

Because whenever your birthday is, the next one is ALWAYS coming up.

Yet, because it incorporates a time element, the copy conveys a sense of urgency.

A real-life example from a State Farm DM envelope teaser:

"If you come in prior to your birthday, you may quality for a $125,000 life insurance policy for $97.23 per month."

Another example is a mailer selling a home warranty that begins:

"This letter is to inform you that your property's home warranty may be expiring or may have already expired."

Again, it sounds timely.

But when you reason it out, you realize that just about everything on the planet either may be expiring or is already expired—including our own lives, right?

Exercise: See if you can find a way to incorporate an evergreen urgency angle into one of your offers.

Then test it.

If it works, then you now have a valuable marketing asset in your toolbox you can use and reuse many times:

Evergreen urgency…a simple "hack" to manufacture urgency where in fact there really is none—only your reader does not know the trick you are using to get her to act now instead of later!

Simply beautiful. Beautifully simple.

# CHAPTER 82

# How Others Really See You

A post I just stumbled across on Facebook said: "Your value does not decrease because of other people's inability to see it."

That's a pleasant platitude.

Unfortunately, it's at least partially wrong.

The truth is that, yes, your INTRINSIC value does not decrease because of other people's inability to see it.

However, when others either can't see—or are unaware of—your true value, then your DOLLAR VALUE in the marketplace suffers.

When people—whether customers, members, students, or employers—do not know what you are worth, they won't pay you what you are worth.

Here are 3 proven ways to combat this—and make sure people know how great you are—so you get paid a fair wage for a fair day's labor:

FIRST, tell potential customers what you are worthy—advertise.

SECOND, let the media tell your potential customers what you are worth—PR.

THIRD, give great customer service, make a great product, and do great work for your clients —and get the message spread through word of mouth.

Yes, there are others ways to get known.

But if you just do these, you'll be set.

# CHAPTER 83:

# Content Amplification

*ANA Business Marketing SmartBrief* (9/7/22) states: "Three-quarters of B2B marketers say they are not spending enough time on content amplification."

Well, I have been in B2B marketing for more than 4 decades, and this is the first time I have ever heard the term "content amplification."

Worse, nowhere in the article lead is "content amplification" explicitly defined or explained—not even a hint at its meaning.

The possibilities for me not knowing what content amplification is are as follows:

A—I'm stupid.

B—I'm ignorant.

C—I'm behind the times.

But I choose D below:

D—This article about content amplification from *ANA SmartBrief* is itself an example of bad journalism—bad writing—from a lazy writer.

Why?

Because the rule of thumb for clear writing is:

Whenever you use a term, word, acronym, or abbreviation that even some of your readers may not know, you should define it the first time you use it.

Simple.

Makes sense.

Right?

Yet so many don't do it.

Result:

They fail to communicate.

They leave their readers puzzled.

They don't get their idea or message across.

And if it's copy, they don't make the sale.

Now, really, it takes you maybe a minute or so to write out a short explanation.

So just do it, okay?

Otherwise you are cheating the reader.

And yourself.

By the way, the Content Marketing Institute (CMI) defines content amplification as "a multichannel approach that uses paid, owned, and earned media to promote and distribute content."

CMI says the goal of content amplification is "to increase your brand's reach while encouraging your audience to move seamlessly through your sales funnel."

# CHAPTER 84:

# Digital Trust

According to Integral Ad Science, 8 out of 10 consumers *do not trust* the information in digital media.

In addition, more than 7 out of 10 consumers say they feel unfavorably toward brands that have been associated with misinformation—and more than 6 out of 10 would be unlikely to purchase a product or service from those brands.

So, what can you do to get consumers to trust you—and believe that what you say in your  digital media copy and content is true?

Well, the most common answer I hear is "use testimonials."

And the most common objection to using testimonials I hear is: "How do readers know those testimonials are real?"

But the facts are these....

First, no single piece of evidence or data can prove any claim beyond all reasonable doubt—especially with the buzz today about "false advertising" and "fake news."

And second, you can in fact persuade many consumers that you are being honest by presenting them with what trial attorneys call "a preponderance of evidence."

By preponderance of evidence in marketing, we mean not just one technique ... not just one marketing tactic —- like videos OR case studies OR testimonials ....

We mean a true multichannel marketing campaign that synergistically combines many tactics to generate maximum credibility.

Such as...

- Videos AND...
- Testimonials AND...

- Case studies AND...
- Influencers AND...
- Free trials AND...
- Ironclad guarantees of satisfaction AND...
- Third-party endorsements AND...
- Social media AND...
- Publicity AND...
- Webinars AND...
- Articles AND...
- Newsletters AND...
- Podcasts AND...
- Websites AND...
- Public speaking AND...
- Case studies AND...
- Books AND...
- Articles AND...
- White papers AND...
- Data sheets AND...

The idea is simply to overwhelm prospects with an overabundance of evidence—much more proof than you might think you need.

And ideally, in multiple formats and media that appeal to all of the different modes of human learning—reading, listening, watching, and doing.

Why? Because, when you absolutely inundate people, then even if prospects reject or disbelieve some or even most of your data, the few things remaining that they do trust are still enough to overcome their skepticism and get them to buy.

Simple in theory. Challenging, though not pressingly difficult, in execution. But you have to do the work—and on an ongoing basis. Because becoming credible, respectable, and even famous requires a continuing stream of clear, powerful, and consistent communications. Not a one and done deal.

# CHAPTER 85

# The Purpose of Being a Writer

On Quora, AG asks:

"What is the purpose of being a writer?"

I didn't answer him on Quora, as I normally would, because his question doesn't quite apply to me—or at least I am having trouble relating to it or wrapping my mind around it.

Oh, the things I *write* have various purposes.

My how-to business books help readers make more money, start small businesses, or escape the 9-to-5 rat race.

My pop culture trivia books are written to entertain readers—to be fun reads.

My ad copy sells products and services.

But regarding the purpose of being a writer…

I became a writer, first and foremost, not for a purpose…

Rather, I am a writer because I love to write.

In fact, I am compelled to write … and many other writers feel the same way.

"A strange feeling grips me as I write," said *Walter B. Gibson,* creator of *The Shadow.* "I do not feel tired. I seem filled with a strong vigor. The past seems vague and far away, while the future spreads before me, full of mystery."

"The very nicest thing about being a writer is that you can afford to indulge yourself endlessly with oddness, wrote Shirly Jackson, author of *The Lottery*, "and nobody can really do anything about it, as long as you keep writing As long as you write it away regularly, nothing can really hurt you."

Now, maybe AG is a curious non-writer who finds it difficult to understand why someone would spend the bulk of their time clicking away at a keyboard.

On the other hand, if AG is considering becoming a writer, I might discourage him….

The reason being that, if you have to ask "what is the purpose of being a writer," it probably is not for you.

Writers don't ask why or need a reason or purpose.

"Long patience and application saturated with your heart's blood—you will either write or you will not," says writer Jim Tully, "and the only way to find out whether you will or not is to try."

Writers write.

At least in my experience and in my humble opinion.

Of course, I may be wrong.

I often am.

# CHAPTER 86

# The Five Pillars of Success

What does it take to "make it" in the world today?

Well, depending upon which self-help gurus you follow, there are either 4 or 5 factors that contribute most to your ability to live a happy and successful life:

## #1: Good health.

If you are sick, injured, or disabled, this can make you unhappy Especially when illness is acute or chronic.

Action step: be proactive in taking care of your health by:

- Exercising.
- Eating right.
- Taking vitamins and supplements.
- Getting an annual checkup.
- Going to the doctor when sickness persists.
- Getting enough sleep.

## #2: Wealth.

Money frees you from money worries. People who do not have enough money tend to worry about money all the time. The worry robs them of peace of mind and can greatly diminish happiness in life and on the job..

- Action step: be smart about your financial health:
- Strive for a six-figure income.
- Build a seven-figure net worth.
- Be frugal.
- Invest in assets that go up in value.

### #3: Relationships.

Humans—even introverts—need and crave contact with other people to be psychologically healthy and happy.

Build the best relationships you can within your family, and also treasure good friends.

### #4: Work.

Have and get a career or small business that you enjoy so much you look forward to work instead of it being an unwholesome activity you wish you could escape.

"Keep interested in your career, however, humble," Max Ehrmann advises in his prose poem *Desiderata*, "it is a real possession in the changing fortunes of time."

Some positive thinking writers add a fifth factor:

### #5: Spirituality.

For some of us this is optional, but others find a belief in a higher power comforting and beneficial.

Action step: Rate yourself on a scale of 1 to 5 with 1=sorely lacking and 5=have in abundance.

Work to improve so that you rank a 3 or higher in #1 through #4— where you can—and also #5 if that is important to you.

# CHAPTER 87:

# Retirement Could be Hazardous to Your Health

A recent email from Fisher Investments asked me a multiple-choice question about how I intended to spend my time in retirement.

The choices were: relax—family—travel—exercise—social clubs—volunteering.

But the list did not include the option I would have checked—namely, work.

That's right—work.

It was the great Les Paul who said that, if you do for a living something you love and would do anyway, every day, even for free…well, then you will have never actually "worked" a day in your life.

Les Paul loved making (and playing) great guitars. Guitars, guitar making, and guitar playing joyfully playing filled his days—and nights. And so Paul never thought of it as "work" the way so many people are unhappy with the work that is their job.

Similarly, I spend my days reading, researching, thinking, and writing for my clients—with writing being my core and major activity.

Someone recently asked me, "Bob, what will you do when you retire?"

I immediately answered that I suppose I'll do what I do now—which is read, research, think, and write.

In other words, do exactly what I do for work—which is mainly writing.

The realization made the idea of me "retiring" seem either unnecessary, ill-advised, nonsensical, undesirable, questionable, a bad idea, downright silly—-or any or all of these.

A recent article on Medium said, "Is working 40 years in a job you don't like hoping one day you'll get to retire really the best approach to life?

"If you're a driven, passionate, and self-actualizing person, retirement from your job may simply be a very bad decision for you."

Okay. I admit it. I'm a writing addict.

And when it comes down to brass tacks, I have always agreed with the great English playwright, Noel Coward, who famously said: "Work is more fun than fun."

Today at age 65, the classic retirement age in America, I increasingly see on social media friends, schoolmates, and other of my contemporaries who are announcing they have just turned 65 and retired.

They seem happy, and I am happy for them. But then I also imagine their day. What do fully retired, totally non-working people actually DO all day?

Even if they love golf, baking bread, travel, or reading Agatha Christie novels, you can't do that all day, can you?

At least I can't. So how are they not bored out of their skulls and going bat-shit crazy?

And then I asked myself, well, what would I do all day if it were me?

Then I realized I would be doing the same thing I am doing right now—writing.

So for my friends who are happily retired, I take my hat off to you.

But I don't see it for me. Right now. Maybe not ever—or at least for as long as I am above the ground.

One more point….

An article in *Kiplinger* (10/8/22) warns: "Those who *lack purpose in retirement* have a significantly higher likelihood of experiencing a heart attack, stroke, Alzheimer's disease, early mortality. and other health risks associated with aging."

Which means that, like smoking, retirement could be hazardous to your health!

And I don't want that for you, Dear Reader, because I would much rather you live long—and prosper.

# 4 Bonus Reports
## (a $116 Value)—Yours FREE

The essays in this book were originally published in my e-newsletter *The Direct Response Letter*.

You can get all my new essays for free without buying a thing by subscribing to my free e-newsletter now at:

www.bly.com/reports

Subscribe now and you also get 4 free bonus reports totaling over 200 pages of actionable how-to marketing content (total value: $116):

- **Free Special Report #1**: Make $100,000 a Year Selling Information Online.
- **Free Special Report #2**: Secrets of Successful Business-to-Business Marketing.
- **Free Special Report #3**: How to Double Your Response Rates.
- **Free Special Report #4**: Online Marketing That Works.

Each report has a list price of $29; total value of this package of reports is $116.

But you can get all 4 reports FREE when you go to or click on the link below now:

www.bly.com/reports

# About the Author

BOB BLY is a freelance copywriter with over 4 decades of experience in business-to-business and direct marketing. McGraw-Hill calls Bob Bly "America's top copywriter." He has written copy for more than 100 clients including IBM, AT&T, Intuit, ExecuNet, Motley Fool, and Praxair.

Bob has given presentations to numerous organizations including the National Speakers Association, U.S. Army, American Society of Journalists and Authors, Discover Card, General Electric, and Arco Chemical. He also taught writing at New York University.

Mr. Bly is the author of more than 100 books including *Selling Your Services* (Henry Holt) and *The Elements of Business Writing* (Pearson). Bob's articles have appeared in *Cosmopolitan, Writer's Digest, City Paper, New Jersey Monthly,* and many other publications.

Awards include a Gold Echo from the Direct Marketing Association, an IMMY from the Information Industry Association, two Southstar Awards, the Standard of Excellence award from the Web Marketing Association, Honorable Mention at the New York Book Festival, and Copywriter of the Year from AWAI.

A former marketing writer for Westinghouse, Bob Bly was also an advertising manager for Koch Engineering, a manufacturer of process equipment. He holds a B.S. in chemical engineering from the University of Rochester, and is a member of the American Institute for Chemical Engineers (AIChE).

You can reach him at:

> Bob Bly
> Copywriter
> 31 Cheyenne Drive
> Montville, NJ 07045
> Phone: 973-263-0562
> Fax: 973-263-0613
> E-mail: rwbly@bly.comwww.bly.com
> Web: www.bly.com

www.ingramcontent.com/pod-product-compliance
Lightning Source LLC
Chambersburg PA
CBHW072155290526
45794CB00004B/1522